# About the Author

Following a law degree, Mark Starmer began his career in the consultancy division of a firm of chartered accountants, delivering IT training. This progressed to skills training and management development. Now, a decade and a half later, he has designed, developed and delivered programmes which cover almost the entire spectrum of personal and management skills.

For the past eight years Mark has worked exclusively at senior management level, bringing about major corporate culture changes, assisting boards of directors in developing their strategies, human resources development policies, and working with teams to overcome divisive interpersonal issues. He has created vehicles that enable directors and senior managers to hone their leadership skills, working with groups or at an individual level.

At the beginning of 1997, Mark founded *Proactive Consulting International*, a human resources development consultancy. As well as providing consultancy, he has designed a unique suite of tools to examine individuals' current levels of managerial and leadership effectiveness and prove it's development on an on-going basis. This system effectively monitors the things covered within this book.

# *Will the Real Leader Please Stand Up?*

## A Practical Guide to Being a Manager Others Will Want to Follow

## Mark Starmer

Oak Tree Press
Dublin

Oak Tree Press
Merrion Building
Lower Merrion Street
Dublin 2, Ireland
www.oaktreepress.com

A catalogue record of this book is
available from the British Library.

ISBN 1 86076 107 0

Printed in the Republic of Ireland
by Colour Books Ltd.

# Contents

# **Introduction**

Have you noticed the huge number of articles in the press and "professional" magazines about the growing need for leadership? A lot of them show the results of intensive research where somebody has interviewed the people at the top of major corporations, captains of industry or "big names". The reports share with you the wisdom of what those people said makes them leaders.

The two principal dangers in the approach are that it assumes that the most senior people in an organisation are leaders, and it asks them what they believe makes them leaders.

I become more concerned with each one I read. The quotes from the leaders are interesting, but when I read them, I find I know some of the people, and whilst they are certainly at the top of the tree in their respective organisations, why is it assumed that they are leaders?

Quite simply, a real leader is someone that you want to follow, and many of these people are "leaders" only by virtue of the fact that they come from a generation of management that can still rely on the unspoken imperative inherent in any workplace: DO IT OR BE FIRED!

As you will discover as you read on, "the times they are a-changing". The ability to manage is no longer enough and there is indeed a growing need for leaders. But that need is for "real leaders" who can promote followership based on commitment and loyalty rather than implied coercion.

So doesn't it make sense to ask the people who are meant to be following what makes a leader?

I have. Over five years, on three continents, asking the nationals of 34 different countries. But don't get me wrong, I'm no academic! I haven't devoted myself to developing a series of ideals and theories in isolation from the real world. I've been a manager with line management responsibilities, and I've had the opportunity to observe and research the practices of literally thousands of managers and would-be leaders.

Principally, I've been responsible for heightening the skills of those individuals, initially in training standard areas of management process and control. Latterly, over the last eight years, I've worked almost exclusively on helping people explore their management impact, coaching them on leadership actions, and assisting them in developing the persona of a leader. And looking at the teams they work within.

This book is written from a composite of not only my experience and my observations as a management developer, but also from those of the people with whom I've worked. I've learnt from every individual — good and bad — and I've seen a whole host of practices that are both effective and ineffective in my attempts to help them to improve not only their lot, but also that of the people they manage.

If you came on a development programme with me, you'd spend your time practising the things that are written in these pages, and experiencing what it's like to really do it. Perhaps one day we'll meet on a training course and you can teach me some more, and I'll try to help you be the best you can possibly be. In the meantime, having an understanding of what real leadership is is a beginning, and that's what this book is about. Remember this isn't theory. It really works if you're brave enough to try.

You have my sincere best wishes in your endeavours, and I look forward to meeting you one day. It will be interesting to see how you're getting on!

# Telling It Like It Is

- At least 90% of you reading this book are looking for an easy solution. Good for you. At least you care enough to want one.

- This is leadership in as painless a form as I can make it.

- **Explaining** it is relatively easy. ***Understanding*** it is not that simple. ***DOING*** it can take a lifetime of practice.

- Just reading the book will do little for you. It takes a lot of hard work to be a leader.

- You still might not make it.

| ARE YOU READY FOR THIS? |
| :---: |

*"PLEASE DON'T BE PUT OFF!*

*More and more businesses are recognising the need for leaders.*

*More importantly, the people who work in these businesses desperately need leadership."*

Real leadership is an ideal.

I was once criticised by a management development manager for promoting an ideal on a course I was delivering for their business, as a consultant.

Aiming for an ideal is not the same as being an idealist, and in actual fact, I'm a realist.

Maybe what she hadn't experienced was that the ideal, whilst tremendously hard work, is totally achievable.

However, on this occasion, my response to the accusation was a little less charitable, but still made a valid point I think:

**"Don't you want your people to strive to be the best they can be? Would it be better to give up and accept second best?**

(Then I got melodramatic:)

**Where I come from it's better to have fought and lost than not to have fought at all."**

(Stolen from the theme song from "The Flashing Blade" – circa 1969!)

Pretty hammy, but she got the point.

"So how do I use this book?"

"With the greatest of ease."

# Getting the Most from the Book

This book is a 100% practical — rather than a theoretical — explanation of leadership. It will give you a comprehensive understanding of why people follow, and it is packed full of suggestions for things to do, and things to avoid, to help develop you as an individual others will follow: a leader.

Read it through at your leisure. It probably won't take you more than a couple of hours, but there is so much information that you will need to go through it more than once to get the best use from it.

Many of the sections are intended as a source of reference to refer back to again and again, and to make this as easy as possible, the book has been laid out in a certain way:

- At the beginning of each chapter you'll find a brief summary of the points contained in that section.

- At the end of each chapter there is a full summary, plus a list of specific actions to take. (There is also a recap of all of the action points in the last chapter)

- In mid-chapter there are four types of page:

  ❖ Discussion of a learning point and diagrams to graphically illustrate the point.

  ❖ Lists of things to do and not to do.

  ❖ Anecdotes relating to the issue.

  ❖ Words of wisdom from me.

The contents are as follows:

**The Need to Lead** is a basic explanation of why this book is important to you as a manager. It sets the scene and defines the type of leadership we're talking about: REAL LEADERSHIP.

**Learning to Lead** concerns the mindset that is necessary for you when commencing a programme of self-development. It also looks at developing action plans and dealing with the reactions of others.

**What Leaders Need to Develop** covers the range of phases in the development of a leader (portrayed via the pyramid model), including an exploration of the move from DOING to THINKING.

**Leadership Fundamentals** looks at the foundations of the pyramid. These are the core needs for any manager, but it is explained why these do not take us into the realms of leadership.

**Management Impact** is about the thread that runs through all of the subsequent sections specifically about leadership, since they all begin with this: the ability to manage personal impact or "style".

**Effective Management Impact** details the range of styles that a manager should be able to exhibit, giving examples of when each is required, and some assistance on how to create the impact.

**Ineffective Management Impact** describes the ways in which management styles can become ineffective, and gives details on specific actions to take to avoid falling into these traps.

**Leadership Actions** takes us in to the real issues of why or what people will follow, explaining the need to take certain specific actions that add value to others, and how to do them.

**Leadership Persona** examines how to promote followership by looking at the apparently intangible issue of a leader's persona, what it consists of, and how to develop each attribute.

***Putting It All Together*** recaps on the major points, including a consolidated version of all of the action points, and gives some final hints on their relationships and on succeeding as a leader.

Finally, the appendix, **How Much of a Leader Are You?** looks at the importance of understanding where your development start point is and the need to prove the extent of your progress. To enable you to do this, it provides you with the opportunity to obtain a unique personal profile free of charge. By combining the information given in this profile with the rest of the learning in the book, you can significantly cut down the time to develop as a real leader, and monitor your progress on an on-going basis.

## Acknowledgements

Many people have helped me shape my ideas on leadership. I would like to acknowledge and thank a few of them here: Sharon Bohane, John Wills, Jemmy Elson, David Bicknell, Nick Wilson, Chris Kemp, Doreen and Robert Starmer, my wife Sharon and the management and staff at HSBC.

# 1

# **The Need to Lead**

Ø There is a real and growing need for leadership, but it's important to understand why

Ø The idea that a leader and a manager are the same thing is flawed. They are separate skills to be developed separately

Ø There's no point in going into this half-heartedly. You should be aiming for the ultimate in leadership.

# Why We Need Leaders

The need for organisations to compete in enormously competitive globalised markets has become a matter of survival.

↓

The pressure to perform in this business environment translates itself to every level of an organisation.

↓

In an effort to respond, the pace of organisational change grows ever more rapid.

↓

The pace of change creates an unprecedented level of uncertainty and personal threat to the individual, affecting both performance and attitude.

↓

The impact on performance comes at the very time when the business needs it to be maximised, when the business needs to get the very best from its people.

↓

Being able to get the best from others means exercising people skills, and there is now an imperative for the very highest levels of people skills — a need many organisations would previously have considered unnecessary.

↓

This doesn't mean having more people who can manage more effectively. It means having individuals who are skilled in getting the best out of others.

↓

People who can provide the metaphorical protection from the threats that rapid and regular change impose upon the workplace.

↓

People others will follow.

↓

# LEADERS

"*I follow most of that but how can a leader protect people from the effects of change?*"

"*Just by being a leader:*"

# <u>Taking Comfort in Leadership</u>

Change has become an inevitable feature of the workplace, but our natural inclination as human beings is to seek to surround ourselves with an emotional safety net that we could call a "Comfort Zone".

This simply means that we like to be able to understand and relate to what is around us. We need to bring it within the realms of our experience so as to become comfortable with it. Our comfort zones allow us to have a feeling of consistency, continuity and certainty.

A change is like a wedge being driven into the comfort zone, replacing the familiar with a discomfort that we may take seconds, weeks or years to get over, depending upon the nature of the change. In the most extreme of cases it can result in "anomie", a term used by sociologists to describe a state of total "normlessness" within which there is nothing familiar.

Constant change means constant damage to the comfort zone and the nature of business today cannot allow for certainty. For the vast majority in employment, this means that the "job for life" mentality of the past has long since departed, to be replaced by a guarantee of a constant battling to survive.

Each change can dash the individual's confidence in the employer as well as themselves, and in such a climate, loyalty, commitment and enthusiasm become difficult to sustain.

However, a leader can provide for these comfort needs by providing consistency, continuity and certainty at another more personal level.

As you read through, you will begin to understand how the focus for loyalty and commitment could change to be centred upon individuals within an organisation, rather than on the organisation itself. After all, an organisation doesn't actually exist beyond a legal entity and some buildings if it doesn't have its people.

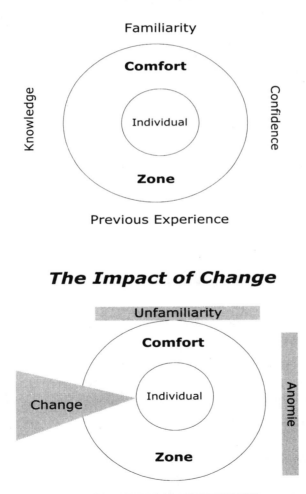

## The Comfort Zone

Familiarity

**Comfort**

Knowledge

Individual

Confidence

**Zone**

Previous Experience

## The Impact of Change

Unfamiliarity

**Comfort**

Change

Individual

Anomie

**Zone**

Fear of the Unknown

*"So what is the difference between a manager and a leader?"*

*Old question. Simple answer.*

# Management is *NOT* Leadership

**Management** is about supervision, structure and authority.

A manager is employed to bring order and organisation. Businesses need managers to provide clarity about decision-making and issue resolution. Their responsibilities involve the utilisation of people and other resources to achieve a series of predetermined results.

**The true purpose of a manger is to control.**

All businesses desperately need effective managers.

**Leadership** involves doing the same things plus much more.

Leadership skills are people focussed but business-based. They are about getting ordinary people to perform to the maximum level of their capability — which is usually higher than those people believe of themselves — and maximising their potential. It is also a level higher than that which can be obtained by someone who is only managing them.

**The true purpose of leadership is to influence.**

Businesses also now need their managers to be leaders.

"Leadership implies followership.
You can't be a leader if nobody will follow you."

# Types of Followership

**You're not a leader by virtue of your position.**

Although a title gives you a level of authority, it doesn't mean that people will follow you. It simply means that they will do what you say because if they don't, they'll be punished in some way.

Ask yourself this question: what do you get from people if the extent of their followership comes from an implied coercion?

You get what we call "MIND FOLLOWERSHIP". People following because it's LOGICAL to do so, because if they don't it leads to retribution.

Now bearing in mind that psychologists have been telling us for the past 40 years that a person's psyche is made up of 10% LOGIC and 90% EMOTION, how much are you getting out of that person, compared with the POTENTIAL?

In reality, you obviously get more than 10%, but the percentage of the remaining 90% you get is based purely on that person's goodwill, preparedness to co-operate, and their sense of personal responsibility or ownership. And that's a pretty grey area that would vary enormously from person to person.

Leadership that provokes "HEART FOLLOWERSHIP" isn't based on titles or imperatives. It's an EMOTIONAL response individuals have to the person who is leading them and what they can influence them to do as a result of who they are.

To tap into the TRUE POTENTIAL of those around you, you need to take them with you heart and mind.

That's REAL LEADERSHIP.

## Mind Followership

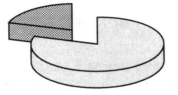

## Mind, But How Much Heart?

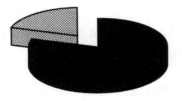

## Heart & Mind

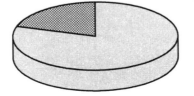

I was once running a strategic team workshop (a teambuilding event done to coincide with strategic planning!) for the chief executive and board of an organisation.

During the course of the discussion, we got to talking about leadership. One individual made the throwaway comment: **"We are all leaders".**

This is very typical of the sort of belief I encounter in my role, and it never fails to ring alarm bells. So I challenged the assumption with my favourite line for dealing with emotional or "shooting from the hip" statements:

**"What's your evidence for that?"**

**"The positions we have are the most senior in the organisation. Naturally we're all leaders"** came the retort.

The heads around the room nodded in agreement, so I replied:

**"Surely you can only lead if people will follow you? People will certainly look to you for the things that they expect from a leader, but they're not the same as the things they expect from a manager.**

**Do you know what the difference is, and are you so sure that people will follow you?"**

The room fell silent.

*"A real leader can unleash the potential that others have by creating a reason for them to deliver to the maximum level of their ability — and beyond."*

# Is This Really Necessary?

---

**Do People Really Want to be Lead?**

You might regard yourself as focussed and proactive and not someone who needs leadership. That's fine for you, but can you say the same of everyone working for you?

And just something to think about: don't you respond well to a bit of real leadership — someone who gives you a bit extra that you weren't really expecting?

---

**Surely leaders are born, not made?**

Show me the birthmark that proves you to be one of the chosen. This red herring has been foisted upon us for years, but nobody's isolated the gene yet!

The real issue is: can you develop the necessary attributes that will make people want to follow you?

Anyone can be a leader if they are hungry enough and prepared to put in some very hard, but ultimately very rewarding work.

---

Over the years I've had numerous philosophical discussions about whether or not organisations need leaders. The argument against leaders usually goes something like this: **"Surely all people want is to be told what to do and left to get on with it."**

It's always struck me as mildly amusing that those arguing against the need don't fulfil anybody's criteria of what a leader should be. A person who I regard as an extremely effective leader once said this to me:

*"Everybody at some time in their lives needs somebody to follow because it makes their own lives less complicated, but in my experience most people need it [leadership] most of the time.*

*At work you can't get by with just telling people what to do. Their needs are so complex these days, and there's so much to think about if you want to get the best out of people.*

*Some of my colleagues have called me a wimp for bothering with what they think of as 'soft' issues, but I have the last laugh because the performance of my team always outstrips theirs.*

*In some ways it's a selfish thing because my life's so much easier if people are following you rather than you having to drag them."*

In many ways it's such an obvious comment, but it says it all.

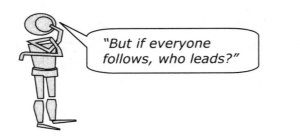

# Who Needs to Lead?

If you believe that the need to provide leadership is based on positions within a hierarchy, you're probably missing a trick. True, positions do lend themselves to providing leadership because of the fact that teams may need their bosses to be more than managers. (And this book is written partly to help stop that need from being disregarded.)

However, in reality, anybody has the potential to provide leadership for everybody, irrespective of their position in a hierarchy. The perception that leadership is something we do "downwards" is very limiting and needs to be cast off.

As we've already said, the purpose of leadership is to influence. **If any individual can influence others for the better good of the organisation,** (which ultimately should be for the better good of everyone) **why shouldn't they?**

The skills, actions and attributes that we'll discuss here are universally applicable in their impact: up, down and across! It's probably true that if you're reading this, you are responsible for others who report in to you. But don't overlook opportunities to influence *your peers* and even those who *you work for*.

From another perspective, as a manager, never underestimate your impact upon others, and the extent to which people will expect things from you. **Even managers who are not capable of leading may be looked to for leadership.**

Consider the responsibility that goes with that. As you'll see later, if you're not fulfilling certain aspects of the role, you could be demotivating people.

Before submitting this book for publication, I showed it to a number of people to test their responses. One particularly revealing response came from a manager who had been in "the services", followed by a period in conventional employment. Finally, he had run his own business up until the time of his retirement.

After reading the book he commented that he couldn't see the distinction between leadership and management. Curious, I probed for further understanding.

**"Well"**, he said, **"I think it's because I've always been in positions where I had to be a leader and it was expected of me. So I never thought about there being a difference between them. I was just a leader automatically."**

Although the belief demonstrated in his response is fairly typical, I hope at the end of your reading you understand that nobody is automatically a leader.

Yes, you will be in positions where leadership is expected of you. But your ability to deliver, to become somebody others will follow, is entirely down to you and your skills — not a facet of your position.

# In Summary . . . .

🖎 The pressure of the rapidly changing workplace means that organisations need leaders to counter the negative impacts of change and get the best from their people.

🖎 Management and leadership should not be confused. The purpose of management is to provide control. The purpose of leadership is to influence.

🖎 I may believe myself to be leader because people apparently follow me.

🖎 There is a huge difference between people doing what I say because they know they have to, and following my lead because they want to.

🖎 All organisations need managers. There is a growing need for leaders.

🖎 Ultimately, everybody responds to leadership.

🖎 Leadership is an ability that I can develop.

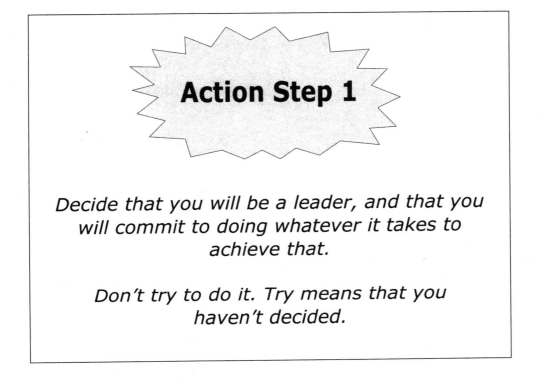

**Action Step 1**

*Decide that you will be a leader, and that you will commit to doing whatever it takes to achieve that.*

*Don't try to do it. Try means that you haven't decided.*

# 2

# Learning to Lead

∅ You might not yet know what you don't know. Expect to find out new things throughout your career, and always try to keep an open mind.

∅ Plan the way you develop, and work at it. Don't expect some magical process or change by osmosis to occur just because you've read this book.

∅ By it's nature, development requires change. Not everybody welcomes, accepts or likes change when it affects people they know.

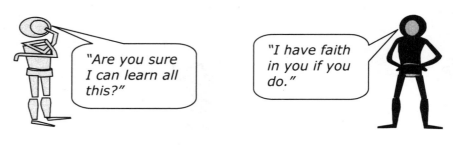

"Are you sure I can learn all this?"

"I have faith in you if you do."

# Can I Really Be a Leader?

The only successful outcome from reading this book is that change results in you from your decision to improve your effectiveness.

In applying the learning, it helps to understand the model on the opposite page which demonstrates the phases of learning you can expect to go through. The words may be emotive, but their application is accurate and well intended.

### Unconscious Incompetence

You may not know, or may have misconceptions about, what effective leadership is. You don't actually know what needs to be done. You cannot be conscious of what you don't yet know — hence the title of the learning phase. Approach the book with an open mind.

### Conscious Incompetence

You will be asked to honestly appraise your effectiveness and as you do so you may discover gaps in your understanding, or weaknesses you never knew existed; or even own up to ones that are uncomfortable. Finding out what needs to be done moves you to conscious incompetence because now you know about it.

### Conscious Competence

In trying to do things right or differently you may be literally going against the habits of a lifetime. Only through actively trying to change will improvement result. Even when you're doing it right, you will be painfully aware or conscious of the difference of doing it right.

## Unconscious Competence

After some time, doing it the effective way becomes the habit and you are naturally effective. It becomes second nature. Ultimately you are unconsciously competent because you are effective without having to think about it.

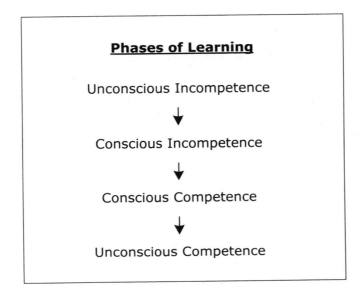

**Phases of Learning**

Unconscious Incompetence
↓
Conscious Incompetence
↓
Conscious Competence
↓
Unconscious Competence

As you're reading this, fold your arms. You've done it in the way that you always do it because it feels comfortable and normal. Unfortunately, you've done it wrong because the government has just passed legislation that says you've got to do it another way.

Before you read that last sentence, you were **unconsciously incompetent**, and now you're **consciously incompetent**.

So fold your arms the other way. It doesn't feel right, does it, because it's different and new and uncomfortable? But you are doing it right; you're just **consciously competent**.

If you keep doing it this new way, you'll develop yourself to the point where folding your arms the new way is totally natural and comfortable. And you won't even notice any difference because you'll be **unconsciously competent**.

# I Think I'm All Right, Jack

We'd all like to imagine that we're as effective as effective can be. Sadly, that's not usually the case. One of the hardest things that we have to face up to when developing is quite simply that we're not perfect.

As you go through this book, you'll probably find yourself nodding in agreement at certain points and believing that you do everything written on the page. Others who know you may think differently. This is because we have views on ourselves that come from wearing rose tinted spectacles, but not everybody else shares those views.

This is best expressed through the use of the **Johari Window**, a model that demonstrates there are two views on us: our own (looking out at the world) and others' (looking in). The perspective varies depending on which side of the window you're on.

Straightforward unequivocal **public** knowledge of us is known to others and ourselves. It's usually factual and straightforward.

There are large parts of us that relate to our personal experience and history that we keep to ourselves so that those outside don't see it. That's **private**.

There are some things about us that nobody knows, not even ourselves, like how we will face death. You don't know till you get there. It's **unknown**. Or in development terms it might be **potential**, we don't know what it is until we have the opportunity to realise it.

But the tricky bits are those things that people know about us that we don't see in ourselves. Our **blindspots**. Facing up to those is the real challenge of personal development. Firstly to admit that we might have them, and then to deal with them when we discover what they are. It requires an open mind and a high degree of self honesty.

## Johari Window

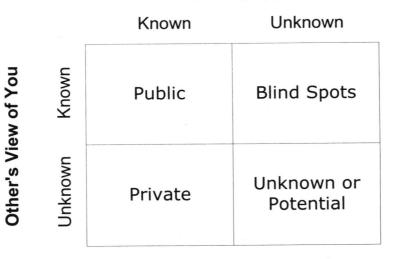

**Your View on Yourself**

|  |  | Known | Unknown |
|---|---|---|---|
| **Other's View of You** | Known | Public | Blind Spots |
|  | Unknown | Private | Unknown or Potential |

# What You Need to Do

What you need to do after reading the book is entirely up to you.
Hopefully there will be a huge number of ideas that you want to put into
practise, and a realisation of a lot of things that you need to do to improve
your effectiveness. But there *are* things that get in the way of learning:

- **No development takes place unless someone actually *wants* to change.**
- **Learning easily gets forgotten.**
- **Other people react oddly to changes you make, so you stop.**

I'll assume that you already have a keen desire to improve your
effectiveness, or you wouldn't be wasting your time reading right now
— you *do* want to change!

So let's deal with forgetting the messages: One of the most effective
methods of getting yourself to change is to start making commitments
to yourself by developing an action plan. It's pretty simple, and
involves these simple stages:

1. **Stop and reflect at the end of each chapter.**

2. **Note the main learning points for yourself.**

3. **Make notes of what you intend to do about it.**

Some people argue that it's cumbersome and obvious, but believe me,
learning points are very easily lost, especially when they're being read,
and this method is an excellent way of getting yourself to do something.

The action plan acts as a prompt, a daily reminder and a prick to your
conscience. After all, you're the only one who really suffers if you don't
do anything after you've finished the book!

"*The person responsible for a person's personal development is the person who seeks to be personally developed!*"

"What should an action plan look like?"

"Something like this."

# Developing an Action Plan

An action plan is a series of individual learning points developed into a detailed set of practical steps that you have *decided* to take. The original learning point that you have noted might be something like this:

***All impact is created as a result of communication.***

You realise that there is an action step for you that might be expressed as:

***I need to improve upon my communications.***

That's nowhere near specific enough, so if you can identify it, deal with the precise area in which you have an issue:

***I need to understand the relationship between body language and impact because I've been told that sometimes my body language doesn't match my message.***

Even this doesn't give you a course of action though. It just tells you what the issue is, so say what you intend to do about it:

***I will study the subject of body language and it's relationship to communication.***

OK, but how, and — very importantly for committing yourself — by when?

**I will read Allan Pease's book Body Language by the end of next month.**

And then what?

**I will immediately begin experimenting with improving my body language.**

But how will you know if you've done it? Your action point should provide you with a method of assessing how successful you've been in developing:

**I will explain to my colleagues what I am attempting to do, and ask them to give me feedback if they see incongruity between my body language and the content of the message I am giving.**

Then finally, the completed point for the action plan should look something like this:

---

## *Action Point*

- ☒ *I need to improve upon the body language area of my communication skills.*
- ☒ *By the end of next month I will have read Allan Pease's book Body Language.*
- ☒ *I will immediately start to put into action what I learn from the book.*
- ☒ *I will explain what I am doing to my colleagues and ask them to give me immediate feedback if they see incongruities between the message I am giving, and my body language.*
- ☒ *My goal is perfect congruity in my communication and effective body language.*

---

Whilst talking about putting action plans into operation, I regularly used to quote the old Chinese proverb: "A journey of a thousand miles begins with a single step". It could always be relied upon to elicit sage-like nodding. However, I did the same thing to a group of Hong Kong Chinese whilst working in Hong Kong and got blank-faced responses.

***"Well, it's definitely Chinese"*** I said.

***"Excuse Me,"*** said one member of my audience. ***"There is no such Chinese proverb."***

I smiled and tried to look unruffled. Fancy not knowing such a well-known proverb, I thought. Perhaps it's from China.

Some months later, I had the opportunity of testing the theory on an audience from the People's Republic of China. Their response was slightly different:

***"Excuse me. I am very sorry to say that I believe you are mistaken. We are not familiar with this proverb."***

So now when I'm talking about putting action plans into operation, I recite the old American Indian proverb: "A journey of a thousand miles begins with a single step".

 "What did you mean about other people acting oddly?"

 "Not everyone welcomes change."

# Responses of Others

Any change you seek to make in the way you perform will have an impact on, and create a reaction in, others. Even if the change means you're becoming more effective, don't assume that other people's reactions are going to be favourable.

People with whom you have a pre-existing relationship will experience an emotional reaction in themselves based on their new perception of you. Initially some degree of surprise usually follows, because their new experience of you doesn't match their previously held expectations. Having assessed your changes, their behaviour tends to be one of the following:

**Positive**
Some will like what they see and encourage you. They may compliment you, offer advice, and even give useful on-going feedback if you invite them to.

**Neutral**
Some may see the changes as positive but regard them with suspicion (because they might not understand your motivation), or scepticism (because they believe that you will eventually revert to the way you were before). At best they will offer neither resistance nor support.

**Negative**
Some will dislike what they see because your new behaviour is in some way threatening to them. It may be because you have become more effective, making them feel in some way guilty or inferior; or your new behaviour may change the balance of power in their relationship with you. Or they may just experience discomfort because they have firmly held views on you and how you should be. In these cases the response is to give negative feedback, perhaps in the form of sniping or criticising new behaviours. Or even try to sabotage your efforts.

"*Everybody surrounds themselves with comfort zones that are based on familiarity, experience, knowledge and understanding. They give us confidence.*

*When we don't have them we grow them — quickly. We even have them about people.*

*So if those people change, our comfort zone is broken. We hurt and react against the change.*"

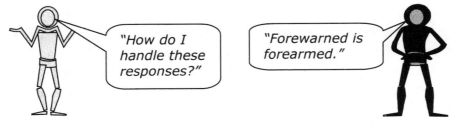

## Dealing with Responses

If you understand these possible reactions, it makes them much easier to deal with. Try the following:

• Prepare others for the changes that you intend to make to help remove emotive responses.

• Don't be put off by **any** response you might get. It's likely to be short term as people become familiar and comfortable with your new behaviour.

• It's important to regularly ask yourself "Am I being effective at developing myself?" You alone cannot hope to be the sole barometer of effectiveness. Actively enlist the help and support of others by asking them for regular feedback.

• Recognise the opportunity in the responses you get. Sift the information you receive. Separate that which is based on your new actions breaking comfort zones from that from which you can learn.

• Get feedback from various sources, and look at the variety of responses you get.

• If you get positive feedback take confidence and stick with it. Push yourself even harder in your pursuit of excellence.

• If you get negative responses, define precisely what it is you're not getting right. You may well uncover more "comfort zone" responses rather than finding things you're doing wrong.

• Regularly remind yourself of what you're trying to achieve. You will reap the rewards long term.

One of the most changed managers to come through a training programme with me had been widely regarded as utterly ineffective in managing his impact for years. He survived on his technical excellence, but was denied the promotions he would otherwise have got because he was so awful interpersonally.

After some harrowing revelations, he "saw the light" and changed dramatically while still on the training event. However, he realised that his biggest problem would be how to change when he returned, and he anticipated some strong reactions from his team. We discussed a plan, and this is what he did:

On his return to the office, he called all his team together and told them to cancel whatever they were doing that morning and come into his office. He very straightforwardly and bravely revealed everything that had happened to him during the week, and outlined what he had learnt.

He apologised for the last few years, took full responsibility and told his team that he wanted to change. He outlined the action plan that he had created for himself, and asked for their input on anything else they thought he should do.

They slaughtered him for two hours, getting (in some cases) years of grief and resentment off their chests, and he related later that it was one of the worst experiences of his life.

Although having some more items, their list of desired changes was much the same as his. When they'd finished, he had the courage to thank them, and made a personal commitment to do everything requested.

Then he asked them to help him to achieve his objectives by giving him feedback if he took any backward steps, and they agreed.

"What did you learn?"

"This lot for a start."

# In Summary.....

- ✍ Anybody can develop — at any stage of their lives or careers — if they have the will and the inclination.

- ✍ Learning goes through stages, beginning with not knowing what you need to know, and finishing up with being automatically effective.

- ✍ One of the biggest shocks that I might receive at a personal level is that people don't necessarily see me the way I see myself. I may have blind spots that decrease my effectiveness.

- ✍ The more I am aware of my shortcomings, the easier the route to becoming a leader is, because if I know about it, I can do something about it.

- ✍ As I read this book, I should become aware of what I don'tp

- ✍ know about leadership and take steps to do something about it.

- ✍ The most effective way to do this is to write a very specific action plan that details precisely what I'm going to do, by when, with what result in mind.

- ✍ If I make changes, I might not get it right first time, and it helps to realise that not everybody is automatically going to respond well to them.

- ✍ I need to be prepared for that, but I can actually get others to help me change by enlisting their help in my development.

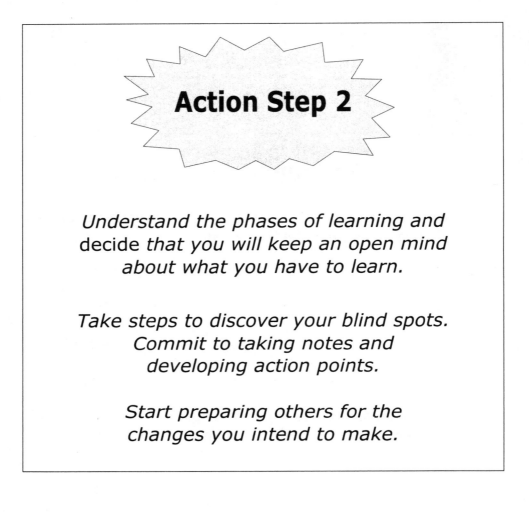

**Action Step 2**

*Understand the phases of learning and decide that you will keep an open mind about what you have to learn.*

*Take steps to discover your blind spots. Commit to taking notes and developing action points.*

*Start preparing others for the changes you intend to make.*

**3**

# What Leaders Need
# to Develop

☒ Accept that leadership skills can take years to
develop.

☒ Don't assume that because you've already reached
a certain level in a hierarchy that this doesn't apply
to you.

☒ Recognise that there are components of roles that
require "doing" and those that require "thinking".
Leadership is an almost entirely "thinking" role.

# What Do I Have to Do?

Unfortunately there aren't half a dozen magic things that you can pick out and learn to develop in order to be leader.

There are a whole raft load of skills that need to be developed over time, some of which are quite straightforward, and others of which are almost esoteric. But all of them are required.

Have a look at the model on the next page. It represents the incremental nature of leadership development. Quite simply, the further you get up the pyramid, the more of a leader you become.

Don't be deceived though. You may look at it and see that you already possess skills at the top, but that doesn't necessarily mean that you are close to being a leader. It doesn't work that way.

**You must have all of the components, top, bottom and all the way through, otherwise the pyramid is hollow, and no amount of — for instance — leadership persona, will compensate for a lack of base technical skills.**

In short, the levels are all equally important and utterly interdependent, as you will very quickly realise as you read on.

With luck, you may already be in possession of some of them, particularly those at the base of the pyramid, but without all of them, you're not a leader.

# A Model of Leadership Development

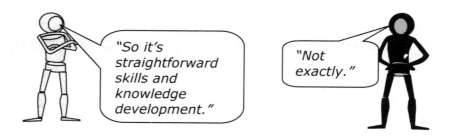

## Management to Leadership

Quite apart from what you see on the previous page, there's an accompanying mindset that goes with developing as a leader that's very difficult to define or explain.

If you change jobs, you get a new job specification and you can see what the new tasks are, but for a developing leader the needs are never expressed quite that clearly. Yet they're still expected to fulfil the needs of the role.

Developing as a leader naturally results in a change in the nature of what you do. How you actually spend your time should also change fairly radically. But so should the way you think.

The focus changes from:

| | | |
|---|---|---|
| **Micro** | ➡ | **Macro** |
| **Present** | ➡ | **Future** |
| **Actual** | ➡ | **Opportunity** |
| **Possible** | ➡ | **Apparently Impossible** |
| **. . . and so on.** | | |

In short the role changes from one focussed on **Doing**, to one which is about **Thinking**.

I have spent a great deal of time working with an organisation that prides itself on a history of innovation within its industry, and it's ability to stay ahead of the competition as a result.

As time has progressed, the business has become more and more successful with a corresponding increase in workload.

Concurrently, their marketplace has become more competitive and they face an ever-greater need to apply thinking skills in everything they do. The staff have become captivated and motivated by the pursuit of success, and demonstrate great personal commitment by working long hours and generally giving more than might be expected of them.

The odd thing is that this has meant a lot of doing.

**The idea of somebody being seen to not be doing, or engaged in any activity that cannot be seen as having a demonstrable outcome — by all — is anathema. Lots of doing is fashionable, and everybody must follow the fashion**.

Ironically, people still recognise the need for thinking and thinking time, yet they experience immense peer pressure to conform to the misguided notion that only doing adds value.

Having discussed the phenomenon with numerous senior managers, they all register the need to break out of what is becoming a very dangerous way of viewing work.

Sadly, nobody has yet managed it and, as a neutral observer, I see a thinking skills shortfall growing at a rate of knots. The very thinking attributes that have made them so successful are slipping away like sand through their fingers.

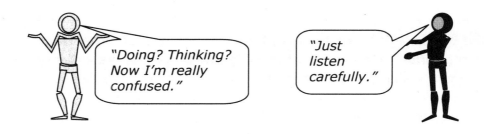

# Doing and Thinking

Non-managers, and more junior managers focus on being hands-on and actually doing the job. This sort of activity can be described as **"Doing"**. It's results-based, tangible and quantifiable.

With a managerial appointment or career progression comes a need to introduce a new focus. Now the individual has to consider tasks that require input beyond that which is the product of ability to apply technical knowledge. Now they also have to focus on how **best** to get the job done.

This activity can be described as **"Thinking"**. It too is results-based, but the results come from the intangible, qualifiable. The extra bits you do to maximise the doing!

**The further a manager progresses, the greater the amount of time that *should* be spent on these thinking skills, principal amongst which is — naturally — how to maximise the human resource.**

At the most senior levels of the organisation, there should be almost no "doing" at all, since "thinking" activities are a full-time job in themselves.

Some organisations refer to this as "working smarter".

NB. *Thinking skills are not about sitting contemplating your navel, nor do they require a Rodinesque posture.*

*Neither does the description mean that doing doesn't require thinking. Indeed for some people — notably those involved in creative work — thinking is their "doing".*

# Role Elements

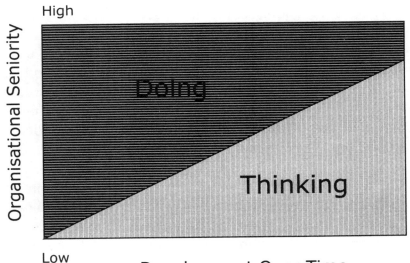

# When to Think

In an ideal world, every employee of every level would be trying to add value to their organisation by "thinking".

In reality, "thinking" is **assumed** to be a managerial function that managers start to do when they move into the role, and smoothly and seamlessly increase the proportion of "thinking" time the more senior they become. The assumption is usually a foolish one:

In practice, an individual's progress is stepped. As they go up the career ladder, managers — in their desire to continue to add value — are often confused by the root of their success, and unsure of the requirements of their new positions. To compensate, the managers keep doing the "doing" elements of their old roles that made them successful before. They're comfortable and safe.

Often they feel uncomfortable with the notion of allowing time for anything that is not overtly productive, and very few organisations either legitimise "thinking time" as part of a role, or have the foresight to equip their managers with "thinking" skills beyond a base process skills level.

The implications are frightening:

- Lack of delegation

- Overloaded managers

- Lack of development at junior levels

- Not enough focus on "thinking" issues

- "Thinking" skill shortfall at senior level

- Morale problems

- Succession crises

- Organisational difficulties.

## *Thinking Deficit Development*

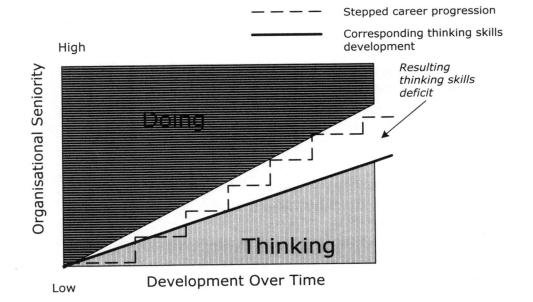

I used to work for an organisation that had a management programme for its most senior managers below director level. As part of the programme they spent a week working on a strategic project set by the business, practising their thinking skills.

It was an international programme, and the region in which it was being held determined what the project was to be. A panel — including those from the strategic planning function that had set the project — would come and assess the results at the end of the week.

At one point the programme was due to run in the UK, and the course leaders went to the strategic planning function for Europe to ask them for a project. It just so happened that the strategic planning "supremo" for the whole organisation was based there, and when he got to hear of the request, summoned the course leaders.

**"Why are we giving these people strategic projects?"** he demanded to know.

The course leaders explained that the idea was to get these people, who would be moving into their first general management positions when their next career moves came, thinking about those issues that would be part of their roles. Preparing them in advance.

**"We don't pay these people to think about these issues. We pay them to do their jobs"** was the very curt reply.

It was of little surprise to me that this organisation was suffering from an on-going succession crisis. This is one of the worst examples I have come across of a dangerous and narrow-minded approach to ownership of responsibility.

*An organisation that fails to develop thinking skills in its managers is like a wilful child who, despite mother's warnings, places a plastic bag over its head.*

*Both will eventually be starved of the very thing that is keeping them alive.*

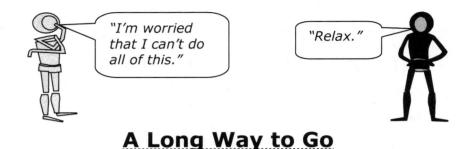

## A Long Way to Go

Most individuals embarking on a course of study find the sheer quantity of what they must cover a daunting prospect. You may feel that way now. However, in this context, you're not as behind  the field as it might initially appear, because you may already be proficient in so many of the skills and attributes that we'll discuss.

Even though you'll quickly realise that there's a lot of hard work involved in becoming a leader, it's worth mentioning at this early stage that perfection, while desirable, is not necessarily essential. This is because there are actually very few leaders around.

***After you've finished reading the book, consider how many people you know who meet the criteria for promoting followership, or how many people you would follow. I'd be very surprised if you could name more than a handful.***

On this basis, it's relatively easy to stand out from the crowd by adding more value than the average manager, and if you take the action steps we discuss, you'll be able to do that, and a lot more.

Considering the explosive growth in the need for leaders, one person who is 1% better and more effective as a leader is better than none. At no stage do you need to become disheartened by thinking that there's "so much to do", because even by taking small steps, you'll be making relatively big improvements.

However, don't let these words of comfort lead you to feel complacent. It's still preferable to strive to be the very best that you can be, rather than accepting that second best, or a half-hearted attempt will suffice. Later on you'll see a reference to ordinary and extraordinary.

**Go for extraordinary**!

# In Summary......

✍ To be a leader, I will need to develop a range of attributes that combine knowledge and skills.

✍ It's possible that I can be effective as a manager without utilising these skills, but to be a leader I require all of them.

✍ The components of a manager's role shift from a focus on doing the job to thinking about how it could best be done.

✍ As I rise to the most senior levels, thinking becomes a full time job in itself.

✍ My organisation should plan and prepare me for the skills associated with this change; but if they don't, my success as a leader becomes my personal responsibility.

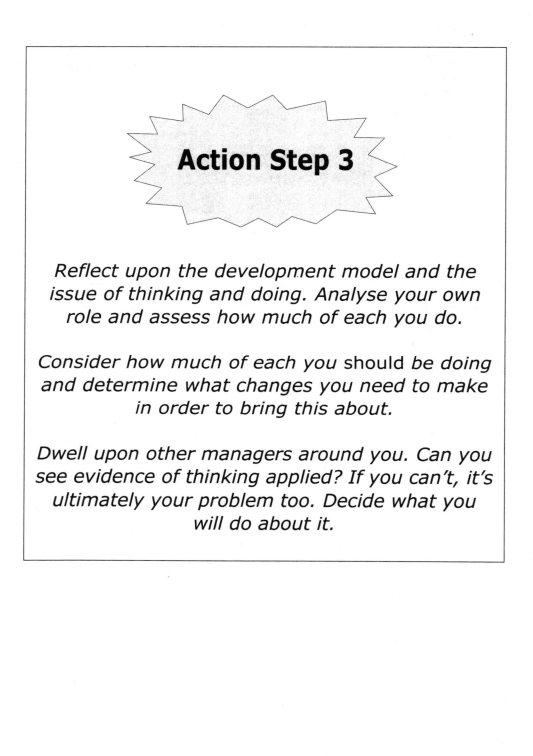

# Action Step 3

*Reflect upon the development model and the issue of thinking and doing. Analyse your own role and assess how much of each you do.*

*Consider how much of each you should be doing and determine what changes you need to make in order to bring this about.*

*Dwell upon other managers around you. Can you see evidence of thinking applied? If you can't, it's ultimately your problem too. Decide what you will do about it.*

# 4

# Fundamentals of Leadership

Ø Without a sound grounding in basic management skills, a leader has no credibility.

Ø These are a combination of what you know, and the way you seek to provide the control that is the real reason for any management job.

Ø Doing these things well will never make you a leader, but you will never be one without them.

"OK, where do we start?"

"Remember the pyramid? With technical knowledge."

# Beginning at the Beginning

☞ Technical knowledge is the thing that makes you employable in the first place. It's what enables you to do your job, and varies enormously, depending upon the job you do.

☞ The extent of your technical knowledge may provide you with a gateway to other positions.

☞ Most managers achieve their first management post as a result of their technical knowledge.

☞ Unless they are developing purely as a technical specialist, the more senior a manager becomes, the greater their technical knowledge needs are — but in breadth rather than depth.

☞ This is so that they may relate to colleagues from different disciplines.

☞ Eventually, as seniority increases, technical needs become fairly non-specific and cover an extremely wide range of issues.

☞ You often hear it said that "leaders know a little about a lot, but a lot about very little". That's entirely appropriate because the mind set that a leader is required to bring to bear changes, the more senior they become. They move from "**DOING**" to "**THINKING**".

I know a director who was criticised by some of his team for having technical knowledge that was inferior to theirs.

Although they regarded him as an effective manager, they could see that he had cleverly surrounded himself with people who were very good at their jobs, and he "rode off their backs"

On an event that I was running for them, they decided to tell me about it in the most negative of ways. My response to these whines shocked them:

**"So what? Surely the more senior a person becomes, the more their focus should be on thinking rather than doing?**

**The real skill for leaders is getting the best out of others and applying themselves to matters that keep the company in business. What does it matter if he can't do your jobs?"**

Nobody could disagree. But it then became apparent that the real issue was that he wasn't giving credit where credit was due. And that's another issue entirely!

# Technical Needs

You already possess that which has got you to where you are now. However, with the pace of change we are experiencing, for how long does that knowledge remain current and relevant?

The biggest mistake that anyone can make is to assume that having attained a certain level that their knowledge is either complete or no longer necessary. Technical knowledge is rapidly outdated and needs to be constantly updated, and broadened. Learning should never stop.

And what about your aspirations for the future? Are you equipping yourself with the technical knowledge that will take you where you want to go? Perhaps even more relevant than the details of your field itself, are those issues that surround and impact upon it.

Nowhere is this more so than for a leader. Leaders and aspiring leaders should go beyond what is immediately apparently relevant, and consider other subjects that impact upon business:

| Obvious | Not-So-Obvious |
|---|---|
| Strategy | Sociology |
| Economics | Psychology |
| Politics | Philosophy |
| Current Affairs | Mgmt. Development |

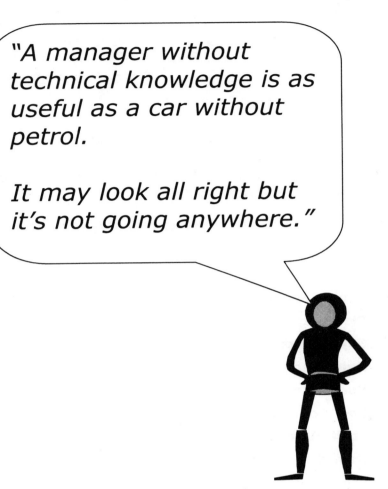

# Process Needs

☞ Management process is simply about the things managers are required to do to exert control.

☞ Since the purpose of a manager is to provide control, these skills represent the basic tool kit for imposing that control.

☞ The toolkit includes all of the obvious things like:

- **Time Management**
- **Planning**
- **Supervision**
- **Delegation**
- **Budgeting**
- **Cost Control**
- **Staff Appraisal**
- **Report Writing**
- **Project Management**
- **Performance Management**

and others that are relevant to specific roles.

☞ Obviously not all of these are the sole province of management, but generally speaking most managers will have them as part of their roles.

☞ Other items not listed above, that you would expect to see included, tend to be subsets. A great many of these would be associated with performance management. Paramount amongst them is communication skills, which we'll look at later.

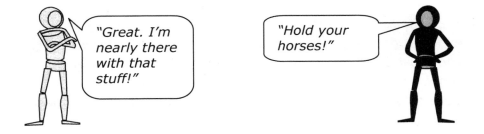

## Why It's Fundamental

Unfortunately, just being technically knowledgeable and capable of undertaking management processes is nowhere near enough to make people follow.

These areas are the fundamentals of **Management**. Management itself is a fundamental of leadership. If you can't do these things effectively, the development pyramid collapses because there's no solid foundation.

Being a good and effective manager doesn't make people follow you. It simply fulfils the organisation's need for control. Think of it this way:

The possession of technical knowledge and the ability to perform management processes are **Base Expectations** that everyone has of their manager. From a recipient's perspective, they're not terribly exciting, and your proficiency at doing these things won't motivate others.

However, if you aren't proficient in delivering in these areas, you will actually actively demotivate, because you're failing to meet a base expectation.

Getting people to follow requires that you add value and do things that actively **MOTIVATE**. And we haven't got anywhere near those things yet.

*Even though knowledge and process skills are merely expectations, and don't add any value as such to the individual, you must do them. They are the most tangible, most easily acquired and most easy to demonstrate of the phases of leadership development. Assessment of your abilities in these areas can also be fairly objective.*

*It is only in the areas further up the development pyramid where added value starts to creep in. But these are also the areas where development is more esoteric, difficult to prove, and subjectively measured.*

# A Model of Leadership Development

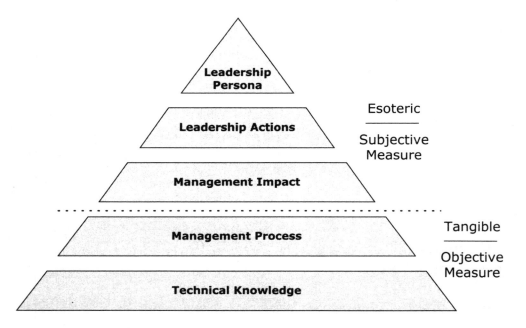

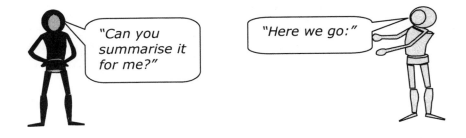

# In Summary.....

✍ The basic reason for employing me is because of what I know, and what that in turn enables me to do. This is called technical knowledge.

✍ My technical knowledge is relevant to the job I do now, and to what I aspire to do in the future. As such it needs to be constantly updated, or increased.

✍ The higher up the seniority ladder I get, the less likely I am to need specific specialist knowledge, but the more general awareness I need.

✍ Technical knowledge fuels thinking.

✍ As a manager, I also have to employ the process skills that enable control.

✍ These need to be learnt or acquired if I am to fulfil the control function to the level that the organisation needs and expects.

✍ Technical knowledge and process skills alone don't make me a leader. They are simply the fundamentals of management, and management is a fundamental of leadership.

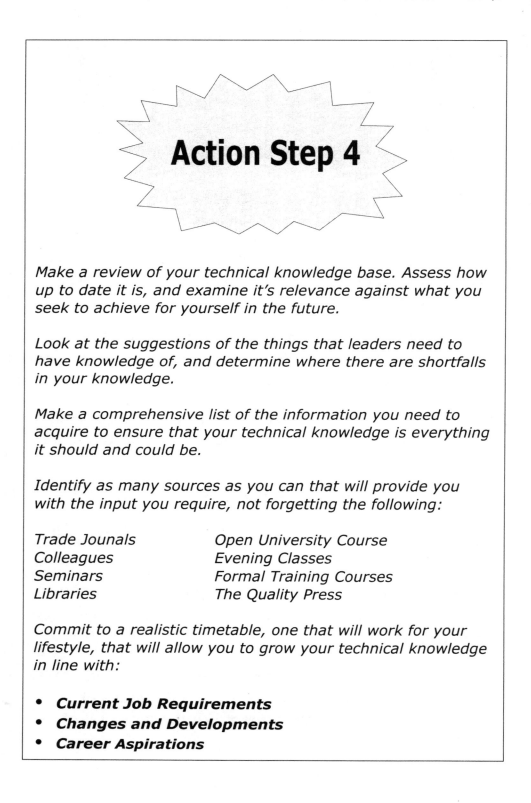

**Action Step 4**

*Make a review of your technical knowledge base. Assess how up to date it is, and examine it's relevance against what you seek to achieve for yourself in the future.*

*Look at the suggestions of the things that leaders need to have knowledge of, and determine where there are shortfalls in your knowledge.*

*Make a comprehensive list of the information you need to acquire to ensure that your technical knowledge is everything it should and could be.*

*Identify as many sources as you can that will provide you with the input you require, not forgetting the following:*

*Trade Jounals            Open University Course*
*Colleagues               Evening Classes*
*Seminars                 Formal Training Courses*
*Libraries                The Quality Press*

*Commit to a realistic timetable, one that will work for your lifestyle, that will allow you to grow your technical knowledge in line with:*

- ***Current Job Requirements***
- ***Changes and Developments***
- ***Career Aspirations***

# 5

# Management Impact

Ø The range of impacts you create are perceived as your "style".

Ø The ability to recognise the need for a particular style and then do it, is almost an art form in itself.

Ø In every communication that you make you have choices that determine the success of the outcome.

# The Development Lynchpin

The next level of the development pyramid is about **MANAGEMENT IMPACT**.

Your impact as a manager will make or break your effectiveness. If the way you go about providing for the organisation's needs (in the bottom two tiers of the development pyramid) damages other people, you immediately undermine your effectiveness.

You are destined never to maximise the potential of others. Quite simply, if they don't find the way you are acceptable, you will reduce your credibility as a manager, and they won't follow you.

Like technical knowledge and management process, effective management impact is an expectation others have of you. Sadly it's one that is often never met, because so many managers are careless of the impact that they make. They disregard their team's, or their peers' — or sometimes even their boss's — right to be treated civilly or appropriately.

Don't misinterpret what is being said here. **Effective management impact is not about being nice to people. It's about behaving in a manner that is right for the situation.**

Your impact in the workplace is often described as a **MANAGEMENT STYLE**. Your management style has far-reaching implications for you as a potential leader, because it is effectively the lynchpin in the pyramid.

"*Management style is an expression of your personality in the way you react to different situations.*

*Management style tends to evolve unconsciously as you master the skills and functions of management, or as a result of avoiding/copying experiences.*

*Management style is measured not by what you do, but by the response your behaviour and communication provokes in others.*

*Your management style determines the attitudes of your colleagues towards you . . ."*

My first boss in my first job was a man who possessed many of the higher-level leadership qualities discussed in this book, along with a roguish personal charm. He was great with clients and the team alike, and he could switch styles seamlessly. His only flaw was an apparent belief that when there were mistakes, you had to deal with them harshly to make sure they never happened again.

As a young university leaver, I left his office on several occasions near to tears from a verbal dressing down, saddened most by the feeling of having let down my leader.

Then one day he went too far and the language used on me was over the top. My first port of call after leaving his office was to a telephone, and the call was to a recruitment agency. I'd left the firm within two months.

What I find interesting looking back is that I had no prior intention to leave; I was fiercely loyal to the man and I probably would have stayed for many years. But the impact of his behaviour was so damaging that it totally undermined his ability to lead me because, in my eyes, his credibility was destroyed. Even though I was inexperienced, and not yet a manager, I was aware of how inappropriate his behaviour had been. A lapse in effectiveness at one level of the pyramid brought the whole thing crashing down.

"So where does style come from?"

"Not your clothes."

# Origins of Style

It has its origins in the path shown on the following page.

☞ You are an individual.

☞ You have unique personal experiences.

☞ These experiences shape your beliefs and values.

☞ They in turn affect what you like and dislike.

☞ These translate themselves into strengths and weaknesses on the basis that we tend to be good at what we like, and bad at what we don't like.

The stages above are a way of describing your character or personality (in a very basic manner). However, it's not yet a style.

In the context of management, you will have had specific inputs into your experience as a result of seeing others manage, or from the way you have been managed.

For most people this means that they will have seen things that they like and will try to emulate. It usually also means that they have experienced things that they dislike, and will try to avoid doing them.

It comes as a shock to many that they have also taken in a great deal by a process that is almost a form of osmosis. They unwittingly pick up the management traits of the person they work for.

# *Style Development*

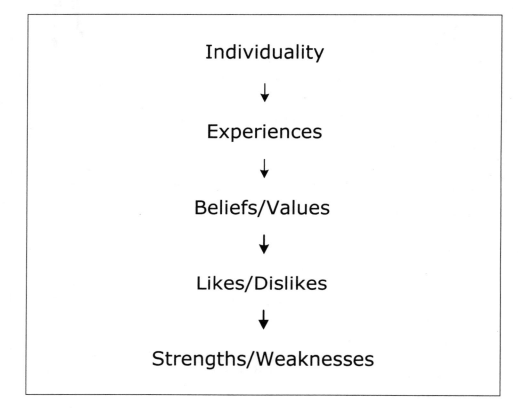

Individuality

↓

Experiences

↓

Beliefs/Values

↓

Likes/Dislikes

↓

Strengths/Weaknesses

At the beginning of a week-long training event, participants were outlining their personal objectives for the programme. As well as these, they had specific learning agendas given to them by their managers. When it came to the turn of one of the individuals to relate his needs, he confidently expressed his own views, and the proceeded to rubbish those given by his manager.

I asked about his obvious animosity towards his boss, and he replied: **"He's terrible. He's the worst manager I've ever worked for because . . ."** and he listed a string of grievances and horror stories about his manager.

The other participants — all from the same workplace — hadn't met the individual before, but they knew all about his manager, and periodically nodded in agreement, shook their heads in sympathy, and chipped in with their own indictment of him. The participant ended his tirade by stating that his boss was everything he didn't want to be.

The event required participants to give regular feedback to one another, but as time went on I noticed a reluctance to give any information to this one individual. By midweek it was getting silly. Obvious learning points were not being passed on, so I challenged the group on it.

After a lot of obvious discomfort and clearing of throats, one of the group confessed that the behaviour of the individual in question bore a striking resemblance to the boss he had so recently been decrying. They had just been afraid to tell him so.

The individual was mortified, but he took it very well, and we spent nearly an hour going over the specifics of his behaviour that were making him ineffective. At the end of the session he was overwhelmingly grateful to his colleagues, and we all reflected on how easy it is for anyone to unintentionally adopt behaviours and attributes, simply as a result of being exposed to them.

"*I don't see how this creates a style.*"

"*That's because it doesn't.*"

# Creating a Style

The factors described so far are inputs. They reside in your head and don't describe the outputs that result in style. Nobody experiences your character until you manifest it through your behaviours and communications — which are one and the same thing.

Your style therefore actually has very little to do with your character, because it is only through communication that people can perceive a style at all.

At the moment you communicate with anybody at any level, you are making an impact upon them that results from the way you are managing that communication. You are actually surrounding yourself with a style: it's totally unavoidable.

But here's the really good bit: Before any action or word leaves your body and transmits to somebody else...

## YOU HAVE A CHOICE

The choice that you make at the point of communication determines the outcome and the impact of your style. You can choose to be appropriate and effective or inappropriate and ineffective.

**PROVIDING YOU KNOW WHAT YOUR OPTIONS ARE...**

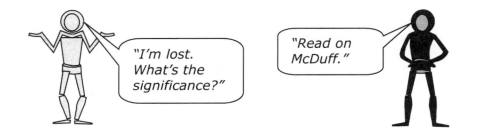

# The Impact of Impact

For anybody trying to lead, their impact is crucial. But impact is totally manageable.

Most individuals who are unfamiliar with this concept, or simply don't buy it, excuse themselves by saying "that's just the way I am" or similar. In all fairness, the things that have influenced your character development have created a person that we could call the **"NATURAL YOU"**. A person who responds automatically, instinctively, sometimes even in a "knee jerk" way.

Can you guarantee that this sort of response always makes you effective? For many it results in a sub-optimum performance that is — at best — hit-and-miss in its effectiveness. So accepting that you have a choice in all things is actually the biggest boost you can ever give yourself in developing as a leader.

Once you are prepared to own your impact by accepting that you always have a choice, and then making conscious choices, you are well on the road to enhancing your effectiveness.

Knowing what to do and how to do it, allows you to become what we might call the **"DEVELOPED YOU"**. Somebody who consciously chooses their impact and makes it what they know it needs to be. Being the developed you isn't about changing your character or personality. After all, you can't choose to be something you're not capable of being. You can choose to utilise skills you might otherwise neglect, or not want to use, or not even realise you have.

Here's the diagram again, with the missing bits filled in:

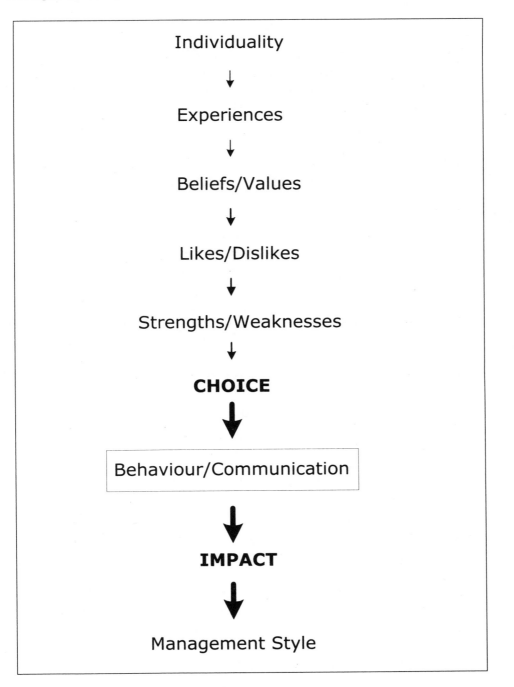

Individuality

↓

Experiences

↓

Beliefs/Values

↓

Likes/Dislikes

↓

Strengths/Weaknesses

↓

**CHOICE**

↓

Behaviour/Communication

↓

**IMPACT**

↓

Management Style

I constantly encounter individuals who react against the idea of being the "developed you". Principally they seem to be worried about changing their personality. "Is that always a bad thing?" I ask, and tell this story:

The very first training I ever delivered was in the IT area — for the original version of Lotus 123! I was young and cocky, and it seemed easy to me, so it must be for everybody else, surely.

On one occasion I was doing a one-to-one session with a lady who couldn't grasp some basic concepts. The harder she tried the worse she got and the more frustrated I became. Inside my head I was shouting at her, but my face was composed.

Suddenly she turned and looked at me full in the face and with a distraught  expression asked ***Are you angry with me?"***

***"No of course not"*** I lied. My face obviously wasn't as composed as I thought. We finished the session with little progress.

That night I reflected on what had happened and felt ashamed. I had allowed my anger to show through my body language (and probably tone of voice) and been totally ineffective in trying to help the poor woman, which I really had wanted to do.

I resolved to deal with my problem, but over the coming weeks faced more similarly frustrating sessions with other people. However, I had practised an "I don't mind in the slightest" face in the mirror at home, and wore it during every session.

The interesting thing was that after a few weeks, the face became totally natural, and even more surprisingly, I didn't feel any irritation either.

Since then I have never experienced an iota of frustration with people having difficulty experiencing new learning. What I practised as the developed me, has now become the natural me, and it has changed my character. But — I believe — only to my advantage.

# The Style Imperative

You are surrounding yourself with what is perceived as a management style the whole time. No matter what you do, at every point of contact that you have with another person, or group, you create an impact that will be perceived and interpreted as a style.

As the diagram below shows, you sit at your own epicentre manifesting yourself through every communication and behaviour that you make. When that reaches somebody else, it creates a reaction in them, an impact.

This impact that is either positive or negative (neutral could be either depending upon that person's point of view). In the context of management, that's style.

The only way you can avoid having a style is to not talk to anyone at all. But even then, people would draw conclusions about you from what you were doing with your body!

It must therefore be better to understand, plan for, and constantly be trying to manage your style impact, rather than just be letting it have a random effect!

# *Style Impacts*

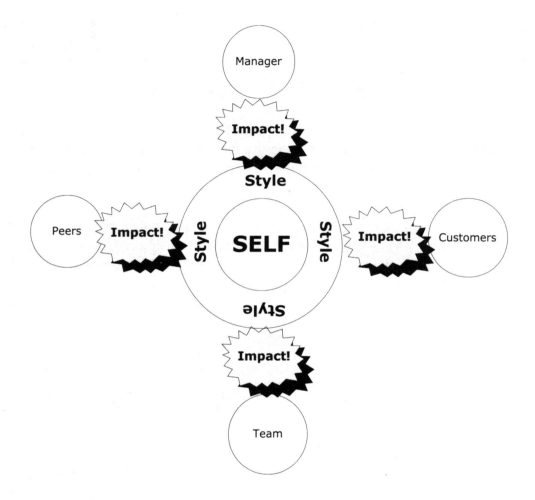

"I still don't see what it is that actually creates the impact."

"Everything about your communications."

# The Style Base Line

The impact of a management style comes from the attributes of the communication itself. These are, in order of importance:

| | | |
|---|---|---|
| **Body Language** | — | How you appear when communicating |
| **Tone** | — | How you sound when communicating |
| **Content** | — | What it is you actually communicate |

Their relative importance to communication is demonstrated below in figures consistently reported for the last 40 years! The reason for the surprising figures is based on the value the brain accords to them during the perceptive process. We believe the evidence of our eyes first, over the sound we are hearing, over the interpretation of that sound (which is the content itself).

To be effective, the communication requires congruity between all three. Any mismatch, such as a sarcastic tone that does not reflect the expression (which is perhaps one of apparent sincerity) causes the listener to doubt the the integrity of the message.

If the integrity of the message is doubted, what other evidence does the listener have to call upon concerning the deliverer? The simple answer might appear to be "previous experience", but every time we communicate we create a new experience of ourselves, and anyone can "fall from grace".

In short, communication is everything. Its many nuances should be studied by everyone who wishes to be successful as a manager, and is an absolute make or break for a leader.

## *The Communications Mix*

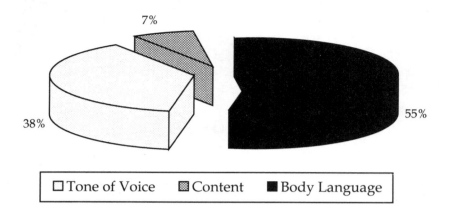

|  |  |  |
|---|---|---|
| □ Tone of Voice | ▨ Content | ■ Body Language |

When I'm discussing the communications mix, there's nearly always a cynic in the room who is uncomfortable with the idea that body language has more significance than what's actually being said.

It's perfectly natural because it seems barely logical. But that's the whole point: it isn't! Our perceptive processes are emotional.

Well, no amount of reference to psychologists ever convinces them, so with a smile and a reverential tone, I thank them for their contribution to the group so far, and with unflinching eye contact, I express with unimpeachable sincerity my profound wish that they will continue in the same vein.

I pause to let it sink in. Then I snort and laugh, and in the most obviously insincere and ingratiating tones possible, whilst looking out of the window and curling my lip, I say exactly the same words.

It never fails to convince. But then I have to apologise and try to convince them that I meant it the first time around!

# Natural Me vs Developed Me

Becoming the "developed you" starts with acting.

Much of what leaders do requires them to act. To constantly be performing in a way that best meets the needs of the role, or the audience they are playing to — as we shall discover later on.

The act is performed to ensure that the best results are obtained, and that the audience continue to be active and committed participants in the drama of the play.

That doesn't mean that the leader has to go against personal beliefs, or be insincere. It does mean that they need to recognise that the audience is looking to them for a particular performance, and have an expectation of the person playing the role.

But it is still the leader who is determining the plot of the play.

What begins as acting can eventually become reality if you practice hard enough, and you want it to.

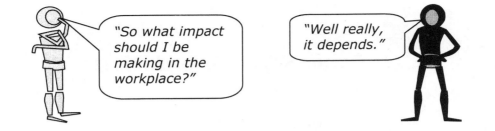

# What Style Should I Be Using?

The impact of a management style comes down to the degree of emphasis that a manager places on either:

**The task aspects of a situation.**

**The relationships inherent therein.**

The emphasis placed usually depends on what the manager considers important, or what comes naturally to them. Some may do all of one and not the other, but the workplace is a complex interaction of the two, and neither can be excluded.

In different situations, it is appropriate to focus on one or the other, or both or even neither overtly. The emphasis placed on the two aspects determines the style impact created, and can be expressed on a grid like the one on the following page.

The emphasis placed should be dictated by the needs of the situation. As we've already discovered, your spontaneous reaction to a situation may cause you to unconsciously communicate in a certain way, and thus create an impact that might not be effective given the circumstances.

Recognising that there are different options and needs opens a whole new world for managers, because most are never introduced to this simple idea.

# *Basic Style Orientation*

**Relationship
Orientation**

| | |
|---|---|
| High Relationship<br><br>Low Task | High Relationship<br><br>High Task |
| Low Relationship<br><br>Low Task | Low Relationship<br><br>High Task |

**Task
Orientation**

"*But how would I know which style to choose?*"

"*Experience, and luck.*"

# Choosing a Style

The emphasis you place should be based on your assessment of which will result in the most effective outcome in a particular situation. Any situation is composed of certain elements, as shown below. You must judge which prevail on any particular occasion.

✓ **Managers** (not necessarily just your own)

✓ **Peers/Customers** (internal or external)

✓ **Team** (those working for you)

✓ **Methodology** (the way you are required to behave as a result of the specific role you fulfil)

✓ **Organisation** (any particular ways you have to behave as a manager in order for your actions to be culturally acceptable).

Remember that each of the human elements (**Managers, Peers/Customers, Team**) in a situation have their own styles and expectations. If you are to get the best out of the situation, take this into account if need be.

Be careful not to use your job (**Methodology**) as an excuse for behaviour. Only in rare cases, such as policing, is this a valid legitimisation for a style.

Most managers are constantly aware of an **Organisational** backdrop or context for their actions. It's a brave manager that flaunts company values.

Getting the right style is initially a matter of trial and error which, over time, becomes a matter of experience. There are no magic formulae or ways of assessing instantaneously.

When dealing with an impending situation such as a meeting, considering the outcomes of alternative approaches or even rehearsing helps a great deal.

## *Situational Elements*

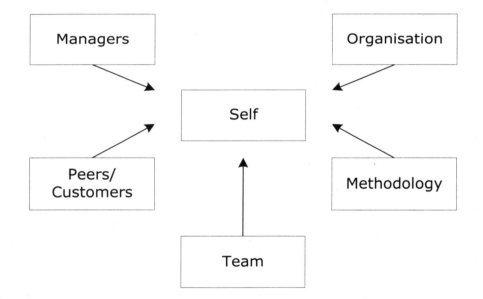

"So a management style isn't just for those who work for me?"

"Absolutely not!"

# Who Is a Style For?

It's all too easy to associate management — generally — with looking "downward", and seeing it as about dealing with those who work for us.

In actual fact, management starts with self-management, and extends to dealing with all of the issues that we face on a day-to-day basis. In some context or other, we are managing circumstances and situations that involve all of the elements shown in the previous diagram.

This means that in many respects, our management of those around and above us in an hierarchy is just as important as dealing with those who are direct reports, or below us. In part, this is because our management of peer relationships has a large part to play in the achievement of effective team working.

If you want to take a more personal view on it, the strength of the relationships you have with your "superiors" has a lot to do with your progression in an organisation. And never underestimate the capacity of a colleague to influence their superiors in decisions that may impact upon you. To put it bluntly:

> **Management style — the impact you create — is crucial in determining the attitudes of all those around you, to you.**

Neither should you think that leadership is about leading those below you. You can also be a leader amongst your peers, and even your bosses if you know how.

# Different vs Consistent

Managers are often worried that if they change their behaviour it will be seen as inconsistent. And actually, yes it would be if you underwent major shifts in behaviour that made it look as if your personality were changing. It would be real Jekyll and Hyde stuff.

But the movements in style impact are caused by very minor alterations in the way you deal with others: A slight change of seriousness in tone; a particular stress on a word; a softness or hardening in the set of the face.

It's actually a very simple thing to do to change a style, providing you are aware of how the movements are made — and we'll come to that in the next chapter.

Consistency in relation to management is about **consistency of effectiveness** — not of behaviour.

Providing that you are consistently using an appropriate style, people will barely notice the shift in approach. If they do, and see that it's the right thing to do, it won't appear to be in the least bit inconsistent!

In the light of what is to come you will probably seek to experiment with using different styles from your normal approach. When you do so, remember what was said in "Learning to Lead" about preparing others, and getting as much feedback as possible.

"If you start out as effective, but fail to vary your style when your approach is no longer appropriate, and thereby become ineffective by not being flexible — that's inconsistent."

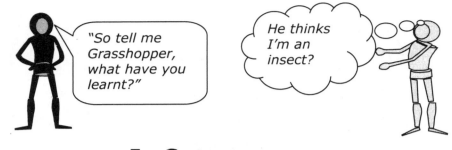

# In Summary . . . .

- The impact I create as a manager can enhance or undermine my overall effectiveness.

- I create an impact on everybody I meet as a result of the way I communicate with them in the workplace. That impact would be called a management style.

- Everybody has the ability through choice to create their own impact by choosing the way they communicate.

- It is vital to be conscious of the point at which my choices are made, and what range of options are available to me.

- I communicate instinctively and naturally, but I can learn to be a developed version of myself in order to be most effective.

- Mastering the impact of a style begins with understanding how to use the elements of the communications mix — content, tone and body language.

- Communicating in a way that is not "natural" may require some acting initially, but that's no bad thing if it makes me effective.

- A management style reflects the degree of emphasis that I place upon either the task in hand, or the relationships therein.

- Different style approaches are appropriate for different situations.

- In any situation I should assess which elements are most influential in determining what the choice of style should be.

- Management styles are relevant in my dealing with everyone, not just those who work for me.

- Changing styles is not inconsistent providing effectiveness is maintained.

**Action Step 5**

*Realistically appraise the impact you make, and look for evidence to support your analysis.*

*Track the sources of the beliefs and values you hold about the way to lead by reflecting upon the experiences that have shaped your past and determined your present.*

*Determine to become aware of the choices that you make, and gauge whether or not you are actively deciding, or just responding.*

*Study the communications mix and ensure that you have done enough to equip yourself with the skills and knowledge to make you the expert you need to be in this area.*

*Start considering every situation from the perspective of "what should be determining the emphasis of my style?" rather than simply reacting.*

**6**

# Effective Management Impact

- Ø Creating effective management impact is about doing the right thing to the right person at the right time.

- Ø To deliver a style effectively also requires you to be cohesive in the way you communicate.

- Ø The same style that you use may have a totally different impact upon two different people.

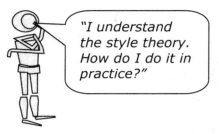

"I understand the style theory. How do I do it in practice?"

"Let's expand upon it a little."

# Theory into Practice

The high and lows of the situational management grid don't really express what's behind the style impacts or why and when you would use a particular approach.

Here are some more meaningful words that describe the impact created, and the way others would perceive your style if the style is done correctly:

**Supportive**
Emphasising the personal relationship that you have with somebody so as to achieve the task.

**Participative**
Involving others in your decision-making processes to add value to the task or increase their commitment. Or involving yourself in others' decision-making processes, so as to add value to them.

**Directive**
Giving instructions to establish the requirements and expectations for the completion of a task.

**Delegative**
Distancing yourself from both the task and the people involved so as to allow them freedom of action, or allow yourself freedom.

# *Effective Styles*

**Relationship
Orientation**

| | |
|---|---|
| Supportive | Participative |
| Delegative | Directive |

**Task
Orientation**

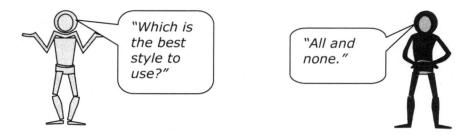

# Is There a "Best" Style?

It's vital to remember that there are no good and bad styles, just appropriate ones and inappropriate ones. All of the styles are equally "best" if used in the right situation.

Some managers do fall into the trap of believing that one style is more effective than others, and try to use it all the time, perhaps at great cost to themselves and their organisations.

We've already discussed when you should use which style, but it's worth re-emphasising that different people will react very differently to the same style.

Basically, this means that one person will respond to your (say) directive approach in a positive and energetic way, whilst somebody else might think that it's usage is totally inappropriate and ineffective. (We'll talk more about ineffective use of styles later.)

The only circumstances where it could be argued that one style is better than another is when you are seeking to manage your relationships with the people who manage you. As you will see in the descriptions that follow, one style lends itself to this situation above all others.

Hopefully it will be obvious why!

*"The same sun that melts the wax can harden clay.*

*The same rain that drowns the rat will grow the hay."*

Amy Grant

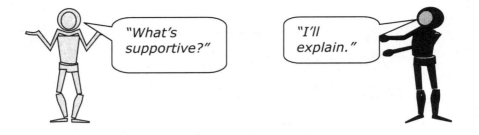

**Supportive**

Emphasising the personal relationship that you have with somebody so as to achieve the task.

Somebody who is being supportive would most typically be described as:

| | |
|---|---|
| **Trusted** | **Considerate** |
| **A Listener** | **Approachable** |
| **Open** | **Empathetic** |
| **Responsive** | **Understanding** |
| **Helpful** | **Concerned** |
| **Loyal** | **Supportive** |

The supportive style is necessary when the situation has a more "human focus" than a task one. These situations are relatively rare in the workplace, since people are there to do their jobs.

However, many managers who regard themselves as strong on people skills will tend to employ the style a great deal — perhaps unnecessarily so.

All of the other styles contain relationship elements, and this should be remembered when a style is selected.

# When to be Supportive

Examples might include:

☞ When personal issues are affecting an individual's performance.

☞ When sensitive issues are being dealt with.

☞ When you are preparing to make a delegation and the person you are to delegate to is unsettled by the new responsibility.

☞ When it is important to develop personal relationships, perhaps because you are meeting someone for the first time.

☞ When an individual is distressed.

☞ When you seek to develop an individual.

☞ When the person being managed responds best to this approach.

Some years ago I worked for a humourless and stern manager. Although generally cold and aloof, he was fair, and could not be described as anything other than professional in his dealing with his staff. At worst, he was someone who you wouldn't feel comfortable going to with personal issues, because he gave the impression that such things wouldn't fit into his concept of work.

As chance would have it, an issue arose in my personal life that would unavoidably have an effect upon my work. With a great deal of reluctance, I took the problem to the manager.

As I went in, he barely glanced up from his work, grunted for me to sit down, and whilst still writing, bade me explain myself. With a certainty that he wasn't really listening, I started to do so.

To my surprise — within seconds of realising that it was a personal issue — I had his full attention. The pen went down, the work was pushed aside, and I got 100% of his eye contact. As he listened, he nodded, asked questions in all of the "right" places, and made me feel totally at ease.

When I'd finished explaining, he began speaking. His tone changed out of all recognition from his usual gruffness, to one carrying compassion and understanding. His face showed a gentleness that I would have previously considered inconceivable. He told me not to worry about anything, relieved me of all of my work burdens, arranged a leave of absence with personnel, and expressed empathy with my situation.

Finally, as I got up to go he came around the table and — just for a second — put his hand on my arm. It was an unmistakable gesture of comfort and support. I left feeling immense gratitude that he truly understood, and that a great weight had been lifted from my shoulders.

About a week later, I returned to work. Almost immediately he asked me to come into his office, and in the same gentle manner, asked me how things were. I reassured him that all had returned to normal, and he smiled and expressed his relief — for me. Thereafter he reverted totally to type.

Whilst he was not a man who I can say that I enjoyed working for (since his personal style did not really meet my needs at that time), his switch to supportive was immensely effective and totally appropriate for the situation. Just that one instance causes me to remember him as an effective manager.

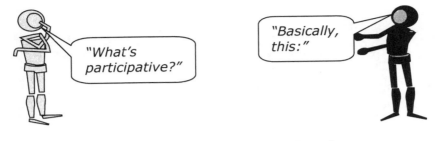

# The Participative Style

**Participative**

Involving others in your decision-making processes to add value to the task or increase their commitment. Or involving yourself in others' decision-making processes so as to add value to them.

Somebody who is being participative would most typically be described as:

| | |
|---|---|
| **Resourceful** | **Flexible** |
| **Adaptable** | **Sharing** |
| **Involved** | **Persuasive** |
| **Interested** | **Reasonable** |
| **Tactful** | **A Realist** |
| **Sociable** | **Participative** |

The participative style is necessary when the situation has a high level of both "human" and task focus. It is appropriate when the situation dictates that involving others would be beneficial. Depending upon the nature of the workplace, these situations might be fairly frequent, and the capacity of involving others to create buy-in should not be underestimated. It creates a high degree of ownership and personal responsibility.

As a general principle of managing people, some managers believe that you should always try to be participative, but this is a sadly misguided view. It is neither necessary nor effective that everybody should be involved in everything all of the time. It is, however, a highly effective style, and possibly the only acceptable one to use when seeking to manage "upward".

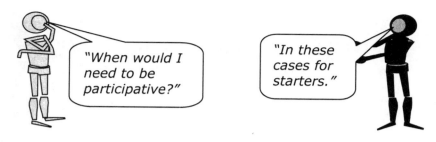

# When to be Participative

☞ When you need the whole-hearted commitment, support and buy-in of others.

☞ When the input of others would result in a more effective outcome.

☞ When creative solutions are sought.

☞ When others have essential expert input to give.

☞ When major change is occurring.

☞ When you have value to add to the endeavours of others.

☞ When you are seeking to manage your boss(es).

☞ When the person being managed responds best to this approach.

A good friend of mine went to visit an organisation to try to get some business for her company. She met with the department head and one of his senior managers, and had what she described as a "strange meeting".

The department head seemed preoccupied and anxious to get the meeting over with, despite the fact that my friend could add tremendous value to their function.

After some time, he made some excuse, thanked my friend for coming and got up and left. A little surprised she continued chatting to the manager, and eventually asked: **"What's going on here? Why did he leave?".** There followed an outpouring of grief and woes:

Apparently the department head had been recently recruited, was way out of his depth, didn't know where to begin in his new role, and had very quickly managed to alienate a highly motivated and committed team. They despaired at his lack of vision, his poor communication, his indecisiveness, his weak approach to dealing with issues . . . The list went on and on.

Then my friend asked the crucial question: **"Have you told him how you feel about it?"** The answer was **"No"** so she pushed it a bit further: **"Could you solve the problems the department has as a result of your experience?"**

**"Oh yes, definitely"** came the reply, followed by an enthusiastic account of what the manager would do were she in charge.

So then my friend explained the participative style, and how seeking to involve yourself in somebody else's business when you could add value was not only quite an appropriate thing to do, but might also be highly welcome.

The manager expressed surprise, so she explained that management styles are about managing your relationships in all directions, not just downward. And perhaps most important of all, she explained that in managing 'upward', participative is almost always the most effective style to use.

Some weeks later, my friend was asked to visit the organisation again for what was basically a rerun of the first meeting. Only this time the department head seemed much more on the ball, and the outcome was very satisfactory.

Afterwards the manager offered to show my friend out. **"What happened?"** she whispered. **"Oh, we did what you said and it worked a treat!"** came the reply.

# The Directive Style

> **Directive**
>
> Giving instructions to establish the requirements and expectations for the completion of a task.

Somebody who is being directive would most typically be described as:

| | |
|---|---|
| **Driven** | **Forceful** |
| **Determined** | **Challenging** |
| **Demanding** | **Competitive** |
| **Committed** | **Industrious** |
| **Decisive** | **Energetic** |
| **Intiating** | **Directing** |

The directive style is necessary when the situation has more task focus required rather than a "human" one. It is particularly appropriate when completion of the task is of the essence and the circumstances are pressured.

It is also the most appropriate style to use if there is a high expectation from the team that they will receive instruction. New, more junior or less experienced people might well feel most comfortable with the approach.

Continuous repeated use of the style, or sudden switches into this approach can leave people feeling bruised, and if it is not your most commonly used approach, preparing people for it is usually a good idea.

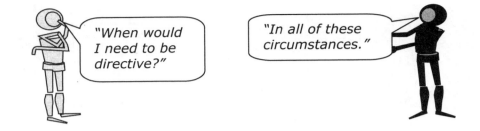

**Examples might include:**

☞ When others need clear guidelines to achieve their task.

☞ When time is pressurised.

☞ When frequent re-tasking is required.

☞ When circumstances are changing rapidly.

☞ When your team is inexperienced.

☞ When a high level of control needs to be exercised.

☞ When the person being managed responds best to this approach.

# The Delegative Style

> **Delegative**
>
> Distancing yourself from both the task and the people involved so as to allow them freedom of action, or allow yourself freedom.

Somebody who is being delegative would most typically be described as:

| | |
|---|---|
| **Careful** | **Efficient** |
| **Methodical** | **Controlled** |
| **Orderly** | **Analytical** |
| **Reserved** | **Practical** |
| **Thorough** | **Conscientious** |
| **Logical** | **Rational** |

The delegative style is necessary when the situation has a low level of both "human" and task focus. Although some people would regard low task and low relationship as not being a style at all, it is actually highly valid as a management approach. It's essence is in leaving people to get on with it, and *not*, as it is often confused, with delegating to them. Making a delegation can form part of any style.

It is interesting to note how many words that seem to imply wisdom are associated with this approach; but they also indicate that it is a relatively lower impact style in terms of the emotions it provokes.

NB: Does it strike you as strange that the word conscientious is included in the list? Being delegative allows time for thinking for the person using it — yet they *are* seen to be adding value!

# When to be Delegative

**Examples might include:**

☞ When you need to create more time for yourself.

☞ When others would perform better by being left alone.

☞ When other's development would benefit from the responsibilities associated with being "left to get on with it".

☞ When staff are remote from yourself.

☞ When your direct involvement adds no value to the circumstances and serves only to distract.

☞ When others respond to motivation through responsibility.

☞ When the person being managed responds best to this approach.

Two colleagues of mine both ran training teams alongside one another. In essence they did the same job, but covered different parts of the country. However, the differences between their teams were more than geographic: One always seemed quite relaxed and laid back. The other determined and highly motivated. Both achieved excellent results, but to find out why they were so different, you didn't have to look far:

Philosophically one manager saw his team as experts in their own right, capable of getting on with it by themselves, and worthy of great trust. He saw his role as one of making his presence felt as little as possible, and to exist in the background to fulfil their needs as and when they required him. The major part of his role was therefore to deal with issues in the workplace that might impact upon his team, but not to deal directly with his team.

The end product was a group of relatively happy-go-lucky individuals who expected little from their manager, and seemed almost surprised if he did intervene, other than to relay information. They determined their own objectives and working agendas. Their work ethos was solid and self-motivated.

The other manager believed that it was his responsibility to alleviate the burden of responsibility for day to day issues from his team. He was there as an "enabler", to make decisions, allocate tasks, clear blockages and leave people free to do their roles. He also saw his team as his proteges who would learn from doing things the way that he knew — from his experience — was the best way.

The end product was a group who had their manager's imposed expectations and targets made very clear to them. He determined their schedules, regularly intervened in their work to give guidance, and promoted himself as the master of a fiefdom. Their working ethos was fast paced and results orientated.

You might imagine that the teams would have regarded one another like sheep looking across the valley — always seeing greener grass on the other side. But this was not so. For the most part, the members of both teams were very content with their lot, and although there were occasional switches these could almost be predicted simply by regarding the individuals who moved.

Then one day, some bright spark suggested that the managers swap geographic teams — for their own development — and disaster ensued.

Hopefully it will be obvious to you that one manager had a delegative style, and the other a directive. Both were highly effective, but only with the people who were in their teams. When the switch of managers occurred, both continued to employ the same style approach, with a team that had accepted, liked, and was motivated by the one it had previously been the recipient of.

Fortunately, the error was hugely obvious and quickly spotted. With a little help, both managers were persuaded to shift their management styles to ones appropriate for their teams and not just for themselves!

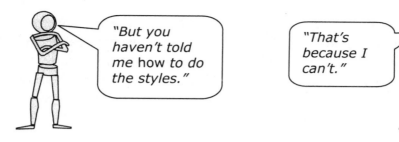

## How Do I "Do" a Style?

Precisely how to create the impact is extremely difficult to relate, because so much of it is dependent upon your behaviour to start with, and how others will perceive styles coming from you as a result of how you communicate.

That basically means that everybody will do a style in a slightly different way, according to the way they are.

Remember that a style impact is created in part by the degree of emphasis that a manager is placing on either task or relationship; and by the way in which it is delivered. That in turn is about the complex mix of the content, tone, and body language.

The content element is the emphasis on relationship or task, and that is simply a matter of focus within a communication, and its subject matter.

The rest is the actual delivery itself, but there are no golden rules to define how to make the impact. We would all do them in different ways, and could all create different impacts as a result of saying exactly the same words.

And then there is that extra dynamic of the person we are actually communicating with. Always remember that exactly the same behaviour can appear totally different to different individuals.

"*If a hamster and an elephant were hungry, and both ran to you for food, would your reaction to each be the same?*

*They're both trying to get the same message across, but the impact is very different!*"

# The Essence of a Style

If you try to think about the essence of a style, you will probably be better able to understand the associated communication needs:

**SUPPORTIVE** is about **relating** to others in order to achieve.

**PARTICIPATIVE** is about **involving** and encouraging others to contribute.

**DIRECTIVE** is about **instructing** and giving and maintaining focus.

**DELEGATIVE** is about being **hands-off** and maintaining a distance.

You cannot really prescribe a certain tone as being the exclusive province of a particular style. You might suggest that:

**SUPPORTIVE** is **friendly** and **empathetic**

**PARTICIPATIVE** is **interested** and **open**

**DIRECTIVE** is **commanding** and **authoritative**

**DELEGATIVE** is **neutral** and **logical**

But there is nothing to say that all styles could not be equally friendly or interested or whatever. The best reference point is perhaps to look at the words that are most commonly used to describe the styles, and reflect upon the tones and body language that would create those impacts.

# Does the Style Make a Leader?

Remember what we said earlier in "Fundamentals of Leadership" about doing things that motivate, and base expectations?

Something that motivates actively adds value to you, but a base expectation is something that you take for granted. It merely serves to demotivate you if it isn't present.

Well management styles are little more than base expectations. People expect to be dealt with effectively by other people. But if they deal with you ineffectively, it's a demotivator.

Failing to fulfil base expectations undermines the personal credibility of a manager, and therefore weakens the extent to which they are able to fulfil their purpose, which is to control. In fact, all of the development issues we've explored so far are facets of control.

Unfortunately there are a lot of things to be done yet before you become a leader. We still haven't entered the realms of what motivates and influences others.

Just remember that this is the lynchpin, because so much of what is to come is based upon it.

You must get the style issue right, or the rest won't work.

# *A Model of Leadership Development*

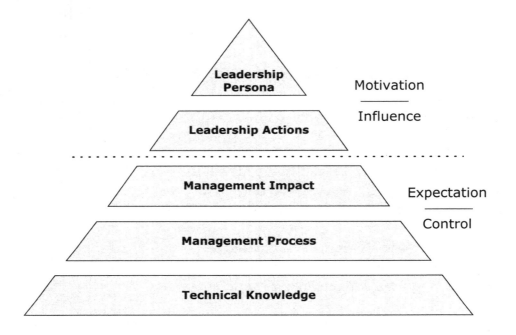

I never cease to be amazed by how much people are capable of, or are prepared to do when they want to. Or in the workplace, how much they will do if somebody creates the environment that creates that desire in them. For me, a classic example of this is the unravelling of a finance project that I witnessed, that on paper looked like a total nightmare.

It promised a fortnight of long hours, unrelenting pressures, and would swallow up two weekends of the team involved, with no opportunity for extra payment or incentive at the end. It was a mini crisis, something that had to be done if a particular deal was to be achieved.

The team worked slavishly, beginning at 7.00 a.m. at the latest, and going on until 11.00 p.m., or even later. One night, half of the team didn't even go home.

The interesting thing was that throughout, morale was sky high, nobody complained, and at the end many reported it as a "brilliant experience". Some months later, I witnessed an almost duplicate project with many of the same team taking part. The requirements were the same, but this time the anticipation was grim.

During the implementation there were tears, stand up rows, walk outs, threatened resignations, backbiting and total discord. The project barely scraped in on time, two people requested transfers, one left within two months, and all vowed not to go through a similar task again.

Oddly enough, the only real thing to distinguish between the two projects was who led them and the management style each one used.

I'll leave you to ponder on what made the difference in each case. But I'll give you a clue: at least some of it was about who got the style right!

# In Summary . . . .

☒ We can understand the range of styles available better by giving them names that describe the emotional impact that each creates. These are:

- **Supportive**
- **Participative**
- **Directive**
- **Delegative**

☒ Each style creates a response that can be described in certain words that people associate with that impact.

☒ Each style is equally effective if I use it at the right time, on the right person, in the right circumstances.

☒ No one style is better than the others, but **participative** is probably most appropriate for "upward" management.

☒ Doing the style effectively is a combination of emphasising the right degree of either task or relationship, and getting the associated communications mix correct and congruent.

☒ This can be tricky because there are no golden rules to apply. It's about recognising the essence of the style and delivering in a way that's right for the way I communicate to begin with.

☒ Getting my styles right won't make me a leader, because people expect me to be effective in my communications with them — as a matter of course.

☒ However, I must get this bit right because it underpins everything that has gone before, and everything that is to come.

## Action Step 6

*Make sure that you fully understand the essence of each of the effective styles, and when to use them.*

*When circumstances are appropriate, practice using all of the styles until you become proficient in all of them.*

*Do not accept the evidence of your own beliefs. Check out your success with those who are the recipients of your management, i.e. those upon whom you make an impact.*

*Remember that you will need to be proficient in the exhibition of all of the management styles. Even if you don't see the need for all of them right now, eventually they will all feature in your role as a real leader.*

# 7

# Ineffective Management Impact

∅ The impact of using ineffective management styles has potentially damaging implications.

∅ Recognising what can go wrong is the first stage in avoiding problems.

∅ You can get by being ineffective throughout your whole career. But nobody will ever follow other than because they're forced to.

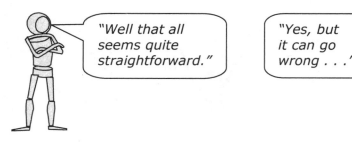

# Why Styles Go Wrong

The delivery of a management style can go very wrong. Here are the most common reasons why:

---

### ● Ineffective Delivery of Style

The most common fault is simply doing a style wrong. Outcome does not necessarily match intent, and many managers who set out to deliver one approach get it all wrong because they haven't learnt the lines. This often occurs when new approaches are being experimented with, but failure should not cause the manager to revert to type. Practice makes perfect!

---

### ● An Inappropriate Situation

The style needs to be appropriate to the circumstances to be effective. Particular attention should be paid to the times when style usage is required. Or try re-appraising the elements of the situation.

---

### ● An Inappropriate Person

Particular individuals simply don't react to certain styles. Every manager has a need to understand the likely responses of their teams, colleagues or managers, and deliver to each individual the approach that suits that person's needs. Be careful not to judge people too quickly, and beware of branding people as only needing one thing. An individual's needs will change just as much as circumstances change.

"*Ignore that ridiculous maxim 'Treat others as you would like to be treated'.*

*It assumes they're all like you, and they're not!*"

# The Need to be Flexible

Any strength overplayed becomes a weakness. Managers often discover that they're very good at delivering a particular style, and it seems to work in any number of situations they face. So they do it all the time.

It's foolish to assume that all situations are the same. Each one is unique and should be treated accordingly. Even if the same style appears to work repeatedly, in all likelihood what is not happening is that the **full potential** of a situation is being realised.

In real time, the need to vary a style might change from minute to minute without giving you the chance to reflect or adopt a strategic approach.

Maintaining the use of a style when it is inappropriate to do so can turn effective behaviour sour in seconds. You also risk becoming what we could call a **style caricature**. This is somebody who does so much of the same thing that they become  the living embodiment of everything that is ineffective about that style, and a bit of a joke.

Thus, thinking on your feet and being flexible becomes a key skill for a leader.

> # You must be able to do all of the styles.

"*A management style is like a tool — you use the right tool for the right job.*

*You use a saw to cut down a tree, and a hammer to knock in a nail. But if you try to cut down a tree with a hammer you don't get very far.*

*But if the only tool you have is a hammer, pretty soon everything starts to look like a nail . . .*"

A sales director who had been on a programme with me was having immense difficulty in managing his team — a home-based sales force who spent most of their time on the road.

During a post-course review he was explaining the issues to me and we discussed the things that he was doing and their impacts. It transpired that despite what he had learnt on the course, he had a very strong belief in the value of a participative approach, and applied it with a vengeance!

He didn't accept that this could be the source of any problems he might be having, so we analysed his role together and drew the following conclusions:

The team responded best when they were left alone to do their jobs. They were all experienced and capable individuals, who responded well to a high level of trust (delegative).

When they did venture into the office what they required was more personal attention. If they were doing well against their targets, they needed to be praised and have attention paid to them (supportive). If they had been idle and were failing to meet their targets, a strong refocusing — or even a kick up the backside — was needed (directive).

However, if they were allowed too much participation in the director's decisions, they made the setting of targets difficult by attempting to distort them to their own ends. When the director tried to maintain a participative approach when the team was on the road, he did so by telephoning them every day, which only served to irritate them.

The analysis was shocking to the director, yet, when we discussed it, so obvious.

Fortunately he was able to make the required style changes with relative ease, and very successful results.

# Ineffective Impact Implications

When a style goes wrong, the resulting impact changes the perception that people have of you. Everybody, even the best of leaders, gets it wrong sometimes, and if you were infallible, people wouldn't feel comfortable with you!

Minor slip-ups can be corrected easily enough, and are soon forgotten. However, consistently adopting the wrong style, or using only one will undermine your effectiveness.

The ineffective impacts perceived can be described in terms that fall into the same categories as effective ones, but the words change dramatically.

In my experience, the best a manager can consistently hope to achieve is being effective in their style impact for about 80% of the time. And that's high enough for people to accept them as a leader too (if they're doing all of the other things we'll go on to discuss).

In many ways, it actually gets easier for real leaders, because their teams have more to promote their followership than just an effective communication style.

Eventually they'll forgive any minor lapses in this area. The greatest crime here really is one of ignorance. If you don't know the impact that you're making, or you're careless as to what it is, nobody will ever follow you.

Here are the ineffective styles:

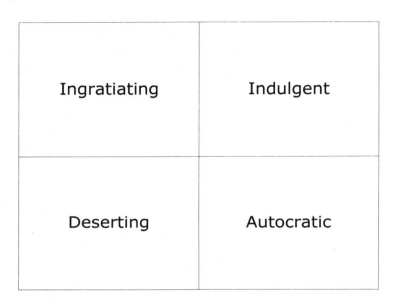

*Ineffective Styles*

**Relationship Orientation**

| | |
|---|---|
| Ingratiating | Indulgent |
| Deserting | Autocratic |

**Task Orientation**

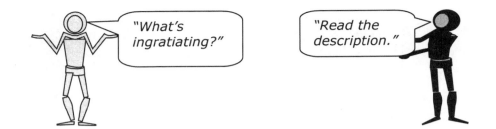

# The Ingratiating Style

> **Ingratiating**
>
> Emphasising the personal relationship aspect within the workplace to such an extent that it appears your principal concern is with being popular.

Ingratiating behaviour is often high relationship NO task — rather than low task.

The impact created may be sickly, ineffectual and plain "nice", or very low key and unimpactful.

Somebody with an ingratiating style would most commonly be described as:

| | |
|---|---|
| **Dependent** | **Pleasant** |
| **Obligated** | **Self-effecting** |
| **Sympathetic** | **Approving** |
| **Gullible** | **Passive** |
| **Trusting** | **Harmonious** |
| **Kind** | **Ingratiating** |

# Avoiding Ingratiating

- Avoid becoming too personally involved with your team and colleagues whilst at work. The workplace is for work and familiarity does breed contempt.

- Keep socialising to outside office hours as much as possible, and be careful to avoid the office party traps — for all of the obvious reasons.

- Don't show too much interest in people's private lives. It may make them suspicious or resentful, or mistrust your motives. The more we know about each other, the more we can understand and respond appropriately, so be interested, but don't pry.

- Conversely, revealing too much about yourself can be a bad idea, especially when it becomes too personal. Although it "humanises" you, it may undermine your credibility.

- With people who work for you, don't become too much a part of the team. Teamwork is a fine thing, but lowering the power differential that a hierarchical workplace establishes only serves to confuse.

- Always ensure that your ultimate objectives are results-orientated. Appearing to have little or no interest in achievement is demotivating because of the extent to which others will want to strive for success.

- Too much pleasantry and small talk can only occur at the expense of the task. Try limiting the time you spend engaging in unimportant conversations, but never to the extent that you ignore others, and their need to be involved with their manager at a personal level.

- When dealing with people's personal issues, be reasonable, fair and helpful. Show empathy, but not sympathy. If you become involved with the problem, you potentially become part of it, able to help nobody.

- Remember that your role is to control, and hopefully lead, **not** to be liked. Accept that you can't be loved by everybody all of the time, and that work is not a popularity contest.

- Face conflict, tough decisions, unpopular news, and any issues that are contentious in the knowledge that the old cliché about "it's business, not personal" is true.

"*Everybody likes to be liked, but you can't always be popular if you're to be effective.*

*People accept tough decisions — and actions — if they're fair.*

*If they won't, you shouldn't lose sleep over it.*

*The only unacceptable unpopularity is that resulting from poor management style.*

Without doubt, the nicest man I ever worked for was immensely skilled in relationships.

He was a natural wit and raconteur, could converse intelligently on any subject, and listened with interest and compassion.

He was utterly sincere and genuine, caring and generous, and he became a good personal friend.

The problem was that he couldn't do anything else but be himself in these respects. His management style consisted of supportive behaviour, that when he did change style, he changed to even more supportive.

Sadly, it was inappropriate for what the function did and for the individuals whom he was managing. And they included me.

It didn't take too long for more senior management to see what the problems were, and he was cast aside with that wonderful euphemism of "made redundant".

I still feel sadness at his loss because he was such a lovely man, and fortunately for him it was a great and positive turning point in his life.

However, I also have to admit that his departure was the best thing for the business.

---

**Indulgent**

Seeking to involve, or allowing others to become involved in your decision-making processes, when to do so only serves to extend the time taken to reach a conclusion; or where the involvement of others does not increase the likelihood of a higher quality of result.

Seeking to involve yourself in the decision-making processes of others, when to do so merely serves to extend the time taken and adds no value to them.

---

Indulgent behaviour, whilst high relationship and high task does not result from the exclusion of an emphasis (in the same way that ingratiating is high relationship and no task), but from the wholly inappropriate delivery of either.

Somebody with an indulgent style would most commonly be described as:

| | |
|---|---|
| **Inconsistent** | **Weak** |
| **Appeasing** | **Yielding** |
| **Over-committed** | **Compliant** |
| **Idealist** | **Pliable** |
| **Ambiguous** | **Insincere** |
| **Confusing** | **Conciliatory** |

# <u>Avoiding Indulgent</u>

- Never involve others when decisions have already been made. The exercise is futile even though it might appear to be a "cunning" thing to do to demonstrate involving them. People always find out.

- One of the most irritating experiences people can have in the workplace is to have their opinion solicited, and then — apparently — totally ignored. At the very least, give an explanation of why their counsel wasn't ultimately followed.

- Once you have involved people, don't simply let things die a death. Keep people informed so that they can see the reason for having given up their time and energies.

- Involving others or becoming involved with others for political motives is something staff are very aware of. The perception of it as being "crawling" or "game playing" doesn't help anyone's impact.

- Simply allowing people involvement because you feel pressured to do so will weaken your position, credibility and management impact. If people need to be involved, fine; if they don't, don't involve them.

- Changing a decision that appears to be unpopular is foolish. If there is a logical reason to change it, then failure to do so is equally damaging. But backtracking to promote popularity is disastrous.

- A lack of consistency in the way decisions are arrived at, or who is involved in them — without explanation — can promote uncertainty and loss of confidence.

- Only seek to involve yourself in the decision making processes of others when there is actual value that you can add. Never do it simply because you feel you "should".

- Constant involvement can seem like interference and deny development. Look for opportunities to be delegative.

The most wholly and utterly astounding example I have ever come across of a misguided attempt at being participative — that immediately became indulgent (in its most offensive way) — was where a manager was faced with the need to make some of his department redundant.

Believing that an open approach would be best, he called them all together (about 18 people) and broke the news to them.

**"In all, five people will have to go. Who do they think it should be?"** he asked.

There were gasps of horror and amazement all round. Not just because of the redundancies, but because of the way the news was being delivered. Naturally enough, nobody said a word.

A hugely pregnant pause hung in the air for what seemed like an age. Then he asked:

*"Doesn't anybody have any ideas?*

*Again, silence.*

*"OK, I thought it might come to this, so I've already decided that it's going to be . . ."*

And he named five people.

Tears, angry scenes and walkouts followed, and the department never recovered. The manager had to be "moved on" (although he stayed in the same company) and the people who experienced this ghastly mess — whether they knew it or not — had their beliefs about management styles changed forever.

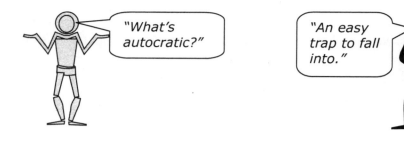

# The Autocratic Style

**Autocratic**

Having such a high degree of task focus that the needs of the people involved in the task are disregarded.

Using language and behaviour that others perceive as personally disrespectful. Autocratic behaviour is high task and has NO relationship rather than low relationship orientation.

The impact often results from a manager having a well meaning but extremely high degree of task focus that subsumes all else, and a flawed assumption that all others feel the same way.

Or it can come about for more insidious reasons.

Somebody with an autocratic style would most commonly be described as:

| | |
|---|---|
| **Critical** | **Unapproachable** |
| **Hard** | **Antagonistic** |
| **Driving** | **Insensitive** |
| **Coercive** | **Domineering** |
| **Impatient** | **Unreasonable** |
| **Aggressive** | **Autocratic** |

"How do I avoid being autocratic?"

"It's not too difficult to avoid."

# Avoiding Autocratic

- Autocratic style has a lot to do with the communications mix. Shouting, harsh or abusive language, a hard and intolerant tone. All these things can create the impression, irrespective of the intent.

- Always avoid physical and mental intimidation. All workplace bullies are ultimately autocrats — and sad and pathetic they are too.

- Recognise when people need direction and instruction from yourself. If they don't and you give it, you very quickly appear an interfering autocrat.

- One of the things that people need most from their relationships with others is to be understood and accepted. Not necessarily agreed with, but accepted in their right to their opinions, values and beliefs. A pretty fundamental way to breach these needs is to not listen. Not listening sends a message that you don't care about the person.

- The workplace can be tough, but everybody knows the basic difference between the reasonable and the unreasonable. Try to ensure that your expectations or demands upon others are based on the commonly held standard of what is reasonable in the workplace.

- A person can cope up to the level that they can cope, which isn't necessarily the same level as you. If they can't do the job they're employed to do, then that's a completely different issue. But beware of judging everybody by your own standards and capabilities.

- Intolerance of dissent is a sure sign of an autocrat. Everybody has a right to their opinion, and you just have to accept that they might want to voice it. Quite apart from this, if you ever try to restrict freedom of speech, who knows what pearls of wisdom you miss out on.

- Consistency of behaviour is a good idea. Volatility, fits of temper and inappropriate outbursts are another form of intimidation, even though the manager might see them as a release valve. They too undermine effective impact.

One of the worst autocrats I ever met was a big bear of a man who shouted, cursed, ranted, raved and swore at his team as if it were the most natural thing in the world.

He would publicly humiliate them; make both sexes cry, and was often the embodiment of office terror.

He was sent to me for "remedial" action, which in company speak meant: either he changes or he's out.

At one point during the course of the event that he was with me for, I confronted him with the products of his behaviour, at point blank range. I asked him if he realised that several of his team (whom I named) had left because of specific things that he had done and said (which I also related).

He went white as a sheet, and appeared to be in a state of shock. Then he began to cry.

The sad part was that he had no inclination of how serious and damaging his impact had become. He regarded himself simply as a tough manager, and his outbursts as commonly accepted foibles.

He wasn't an unpleasant man, and over the time that I knew him, I found him to be extremely gentle and caring. But he wasn't able to change his behaviour quickly enough for the workplace that was sponsoring his development and ultimately he was "moved on".

# The Deserting Style

**Deserting**

Appearing to have so little interest in either the well-being of the task or the people involved that no value is added.

Being so careless as to the success of the task or the welfare of those involved as to appear to be an active saboteur — whether intentionally or otherwise.

Deserting behaviour is NO task and NO relationship rather than low task and low relationship.

The impact can result actively or passively. A manager can give this impression because of the things they say and do, or simply as a result of the attitudes they appear to hold that others judge from what they don't say and do.

Somebody with a deserting style would most commonly be described as:

| | |
|---|---|
| **Awkward** | **Negative** |
| **Resistant** | **Difficult** |
| **Detached** | **Unconcerned** |
| **Unoriginal** | **Uncooperative** |
| **Obstructive** | **Uncommunicative** |
| **Stubborn** | **Uninterested** |

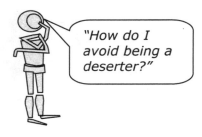
"How do I avoid being a deserter?"

"Heed the warnings:"

# Avoiding Deserting

- Deserting impact is not necessarily literally that, but unexplained absences leave people wondering what's going on. If you haven't taken the time and trouble to explain it to them, the chances are that they'll either conclude that something bad is happening, or that you simply don't care.

- Even when you are physically present, presenting an image of one who is easily distracted or disinterested in any way is very negative. Try to ensure that you give everybody your full attention.

- On the same theme, spread your attention equally amongst your team. This may not always be possible, but people quickly perceive that they are less favoured, and petty jealousies can result.

- Expectations of a manager are usually high. After all, if they've got the position, there must be a valid reason for it. So failing to contribute or to add value is a sure sign of ineffectiveness.

- Apparently motiveless resistance to change, or indeed truculence in any matter can blow an impact. Consider what people want from their managers and you will probably come up with a description of positiveness. And if you don't, you're not being realistic, you're just trying to excuse yourself.

- Remember that a team takes its lead from the individual who's meant to be the leader. Beware of the impact that any negativity on your part will have on your team, because it will very quickly become a part of their behaviour.

- Avoid any kind of attitude that your colleagues might perceive as toxic. Whilst negativity can have a toxic effect upon others, those who possess positive antibodies often react against toxicity by trying to expel it from their presence!

I heard this story recounted on a programme that I was running in Malaysia on the day it actually happened:

A woman went into a branch of a bank and was disappointed to find long queues waiting. Only two service counters were open and the progress was very slow. As the woman got closer to the counter, she was surprised to see that the two individuals behind the desks were chatting with one another, and seemed oblivious to the needs of their customers. Behind the counter, there were other members of the bank's staff chatting to one another with "Till Closed" signs in front of their windows.

After waiting for nearly twenty minutes, the woman spotted a man who was obviously in some position of authority surveying the scene, but with apparent lack of concern. In desperation she abandoned her place in the queue and went over to him.

**"Excuse me. Do you realise that I've been queuing here for twenty minutes and only three people have been served? Your staff who are supposed to be dealing with customers are just sitting there talking. And there are those others behind the counter who aren't doing anything at all. Can you please do something about it?"**

The woman expect a contrite response and instant action, so she was flabbergasted by his response. He regarded her disdainfully, then with a tone bordering on contempt said: **"Excuse me madam, I am the supervisor."** And with that he walked away.

Needless to say, the woman was almost in shock, but rejoined the queue and was served another fifteen minutes later. But when she arrived at the counter, she changed her intended course of action and closed her account. Then she made sure that every one of her friends — and indeed anybody she encountered — knew of how appalling the bank had been. With pride she reported that several had closed their accounts in sympathetic disgust!

Its implications are frightening for the organisation that it's about, and it shows how damaging deserting behaviour can be. The staff were deserting their customers, probably because their manager has deserted his accountabilities in managing them.

The story is so bad that I couldn't believe it was true, so I visited the branch and sat observing for half an hour. It was just as the woman said.

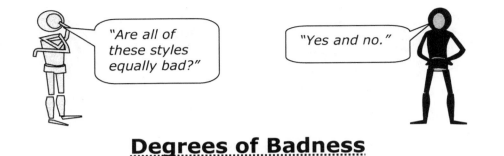

# Degrees of Badness

An ineffective management style is ineffective whichever way you look at it. The real issue is how much they damage the manager personally, or the organisation.

## The Organisation's Perspective

> 👎 Deserting behaviour has the potential to cripple an organisation because that sort of approach can become toxic and infect others. The deserter becomes either a passive or an active saboteur.
>
> 👎 Autocrats are apparently least damaging because they usually get the job done. However, the damage they can do to their team along the way can ultimately prove to be very costly.
>
> 👎 The other two are pretty much the same. Indulgence leads to time wasting and possibly a weak perception of management. Ingratiating doesn't really achieve anything positive or overtly negative.

## The Manager's Personal Perspective

> 👎 An autocrat may initially be respected for their firm approach, but when constantly applied it becomes very wearing and leads to the manager becoming unpopular and possibly feared, making it most personally damaging.
>
> 👎 The least damaging is ingratiating, if only because people tend to like the personal approach. But that very much depends on the task focus of the individual being managed, or how syrupy the ingratiating behaviour becomes.
>
> 👎 Generally speaking people don't realise they're being infected by a deserter if they're that way inclined themselves, and indulgent managers present an opportunity for involvement that isn't necessarily perceived as weakness by all.

# Is Ineffective Ever Acceptable?

Ineffective use of style isn't automatically disastrous. As we've already said, if your technical knowledge and management process is good, you will still achieve.

Many managers succeed in the pursuit of their careers, whilst still being extraordinarily ineffective in their use of styles. It's a tragedy for two reasons:

1. **They're failing to fulfil their own potential by getting by with second best, perhaps doing an acceptable or a good job rather than an extraordinary job. They'll never become leaders that way.**

2. **They're undoubtedly failing to maximise the potential that their people have by not getting the best out of them for their organisations.**

It's all too easy to imagine that somebody is doing a good job, but against what criteria? Often senior managers are surprised when a new person comes into a role because of the difference they make to productivity, or efficiency, or morale, or whatever. Yet the people doing the jobs haven't been changed, just the manager.

Suddenly the potential is realised, when it had been assumed that the previous manager had been doing a good job.

When faced with the issue of ineffective style many point to their apparent success as justification for continued use of an inappropriate approach.

But in the workplace people have very little choice but to accept the behaviour of their immediate superiors — it's either that or leave. Their acquiescence doesn't make it right, or appropriate, or effective.

When I'm talking to a group about effective management styles I go through them one by one, describing the impact each one creates, then outline the sorts of situations in which it would be appropriate to use that style.

I usually have a bit of fun at the end by asking which one is the best style, and invariably (if anyone does get it wrong) get the reply that the participative style is the best approach.

However, I was once going through this format, and then moved on to the next section that was about the ineffective styles. Again I outlined the impact created, but was halted in my tracks when a member of the audience put up his hand, and in all seriousness said:

***"Excuse me, but aren't you going to tell us the situations where it would be appropriate to do these?"***

It took almost a full five minutes for the audience to calm down and the hysterical laughter to cease.

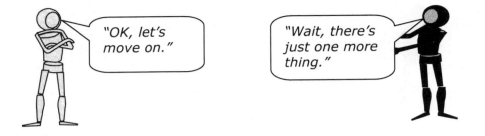

## A Final Word on Ineffectiveness

It's possible to have such a low impact as a manager that people don't perceive you to have a style at all.

They can't tell from one minute to another whether you are focusing on task or relationship or whatever.

This situation usually results from weak or ineffectual communication.

You may or may not have seen it in your experience of managers, but if you wanted a good media example of it, the character who is the cardigan-wearing editor of Globelink News in Channel 4's "Drop The Dead Donkey" is a perfect example.

He's called George, and for this reason, I call this non-style ineffectiveness:

## George Syndrome

Apologies to everybody called George.

It's actually very serious, since it totally undermines the credibility of the manager. It opens up a credibility gap that has little to do with knowledge or process skills.

# In Summary . . . .

- ✗ My management style can be wrong for a number of reasons:
    - I simply don't communicate effectively.
    - I'm using the style in an inappropriate situation.
    - The person I'm using it on doesn't need that style

- ✗ I should beware of trying to repeat the styles I'm best at in all situations, because no two situations are alike.

- ✗ Getting a style wrong isn't the end of the world, provided I learn from my mistakes.

- ✗ The change from effective use of a style to ineffective use changes the impact totally, and the styles now become:
    - **Ingratiating**
    - **Indulgent**
    - **Autocratic**
    - **Deserting**

- ✗ There are certain things that I might do that would create these impacts, and understanding what they are can help me avoid doing them.

- ✗ All of the ineffective styles are bad, but some are more damaging than others.

- ✗ Ironically, I can be ineffective and succeed, but I won't fulfil my potential, maximise the abilities of those around me to best assist in the organisation's development, or become a leader.

- ✗ If my impact is so weak that people cannot discern any style at all, I will be displaying what we can call **"George syndrome"**.

# Action Step 7

*Avoid making the mistakes that turn an effective style into an ineffective one.*

*Make sure that you fully understand the essence of each of the ineffective styles, and why the impact occurs.*

*Ensure that you do not fall into any of the traps by following the guidance on what not to do.*

*Check for possible lapses by requesting immediate feedback from those who are the recipients of your management, i.e. those upon whom you make an impact.*

**8**

# Leadership Actions

☒ There are specific actions that a leader takes that set them apart from managers.

☒ They all require extra effort, thought and application.

☒ You don't have to do all of them all of the time, but they are totally interdependent and require a great deal of thought and attention.

"So how do we get people to follow?"

"I thought you'd never ask."

# Promoting Followership

Everything that we've talked about so far has revolved around the basics: that which makes a manager a good manager.

We know that you can't be a leader without being a good manager first, so it's all valid, but it won't make people follow you. People follow because of two basic reasons:

> **They want to**
>
> **They have to**

Everybody in a hierarchy has to, but if they "want to", the "have to" is very quickly forgotten. They want to if there's something in it for them, some benefit, some reward, some added value. That's what motivates them.

Tangibles that come from the workplace — like money — provide this kind of reward, but do not buy loyalty to the individual. They do not promote followership in the sense we have discussed it here.

To get somebody to follow you — for the leader that you would like to be — requires you personally, as a result of what you do and who you are, to provide them with added value. You must be the active motivator. **That means progressing from what is ordinary to what is extraordinary.**

And that starts with a series of actions that are quite unrelated to management process: **LEADERSHIP ACTIONS.**

# A Model of Leadership Development

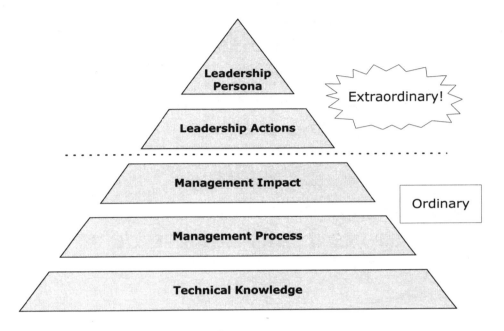

*"If someone will follow you, they have a reason to want to do so.*

*You provide them with something that's of value to them.*

*For a real leader this results from what you do and who you are."*

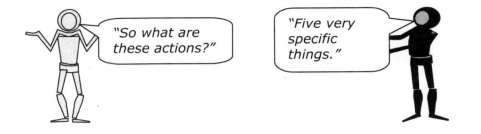

# Leadership Actions

Leadership actions are the specific things that a manager needs to do that will have the effect of setting them apart from the "run of the mill" manager.

They are actions that go beyond what you would rightly expect from somebody who is a manager. They are therefore not base expectations (and so failing to do them will not demotivate).

**Each one, for its own reason adds value to somebody else.**

**They are therefore active motivators.**

Being the recipient of them would cause you to be favourably disposed towards the person who took the action.

Because they're out of the ordinary, they naturally require an extra effort on the part of the manager. That's why so few managers actually do them.

Yet despite all that, they're relatively easy to do, and reap huge rewards. All of them need to be done, but not all circumstances require every one of them.

Here they are in no particular order of importance:

## *Leadership Actions*

☑  Be Visible

☑  Sell

☑  Create a Safe & Trusting
    Environment

☑  Offer Autonomy

☑  Train & Develop

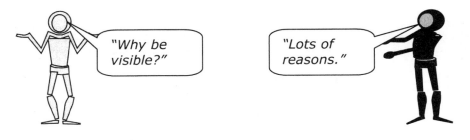

## <u>Why Be Visible?</u>

People like to know who's in charge.

* They like it to be clear about who to go to with difficulties or queries, or for arbitration or conflict **resolution**.

* They like to know that someone is "**steering the ship**", is looking after their interests and securing their well-being.

* They like to **communicate** with their boss because it makes them feel significant and valued.

* They like to **receive information** from somebody who they feel is a knowledgeable and informed source.

* They want to know and have **tangible evidence** that there is somebody who is taking the lead, if only — for some — because it relieves them of the burden of feeling that they have some responsibility.

* Because they want a **focal point** who will fulfil these needs, and evidence of that person's actions, the leader has to maintain **VISIBILITY**.

This doesn't necessarily mean a physical presence. Visibility for a leader is just as much about leaving people with the confidence that someone is there and doing all of these things. Up to a point, the issue of how well they're doing it can almost become a secondary consideration, as long as there is someone.

Think about politics. You might not like how the country's being run, but you'd feel a whole lot worse if you didn't know that there was somebody running it. Not without good reason are politicians, and particularly their leaders, very, very visible.

# How to Be Visible

- Take time to talk to the members of you team — however big it is — individually whenever possible.

- Meet with the whole team, department or business — whichever is relevant to your position — and talk to them about the issues that affect everyone.

- Walk around the office, and let people see you. Do it purposefully, rather than wandering, and do it spontaneously, not at a specific time of the day.

- Attend as many work related social events and functions as you can. You don't have to stay for the whole event. Just show your face and make sure everybody sees it.

- Where time permits, offer to come along to meetings where your attendance would be valued, even if it is not strictly necessary. Avoid the temptation to interfere lest you undermine the position of the meeting's sponsor (and become **Indulgent**).

- Where possible, initiate your own contact with groups or individuals rather than leaving it to someone else like a secretary. It will make them feel that they are more important to you.

- When you are out of the office for a prolonged period, talk to as many people as possible by telephone, or send messages to be relayed by others.

- Utilise in-house magazines etc to ensure that what you do gets publicity and that everyone knows who you are — but make sure that it doesn't appear to be an ego trip.

Several years ago I remember discussing leadership with a personnel director. He was fairly uninterested in the subject, but when we got to visibility he suddenly livened up and enthusiastically affirmed his belief in the importance of it. He assured me that he understood its significance only too well, and took appropriate steps to ensure that everybody knew him.

Some while later, I was working with a group from his business, and, over lunch, they were discussing their board of directors. The discussion soon turned to the man from personnel. They began to relate how every Friday at exactly 3.00 p.m. he would appear in the offices and walk around people's desks. He would stroll along with his hands behind his back, studying people's backs. Then at random intervals he would stop, sit on a desk, lean forward so that his face was very close to the face of the occupant, and say, "I'm John Smith [name changed]. Are you happy working for us?" He would visit three people each week, always ask the same question, and the walkabout would never last more than ten minutes.

The group fell about with laughter as they told the story. All of them had been the recipients of this unusual form of visibility, and one had even been in his office one Friday when he'd interrupted their meeting saying it was time for his walkabout. Naturally, the workforce got to know of these visits, and actually started a weekly sweepstake about whose desks he would sit on that week!

The sad thing was that the director had become something of a joke as a result of this apparently well intended action. His motives were seen as wholly insincere, and many more junior staff found his interrogative style quite intimidating. The end result was that he was a figure who was regarded with suspicion and mistrust, and was by no stretch of the imagination a leader.

This is a classic example of someone that latched on to one good idea about leadership and pursued it — ineffectively — without developing, considering or understanding the other equally important factors. Although it is important, if visibility is to be effective it requires a great deal more than just being seen.

# Why Sell?

The purpose of leadership is to influence. A leader influences people to give their best. To be as extraordinary as they can.

People are motivated when there's something that's in it for them. How does working hard and giving a lot of effort to the entity of a business provide something of value to the average employee? If you think about it, you'll certainly come up with an answer, but it might not be the conclusion that would naturally spring into the heads of your team.

In the context of leadership, selling is therefore about constantly providing the reason for people to continue giving their utmost, and influencing them to believe that there is something of value in it for them.

Selling can be defined as gaining commitment to benefits. Committing to the benefits accruing to hard work requires a good sales pitch. This is simply another way of delivering something called "motivating".

You are selling others on you, your ideas, and your beliefs and objectives; on making a commitment to the things you stand for and what you want them to achieve.

If they buy the package, you're already leading. You might not have got 100% commitment, because this requires other things as well, but at least you're on the way.

After nearly a week of working with a group to try and resolve some of their issues, we had already had many heated debates and intra-group confrontation.

In an attempt to quantify the causes of some of their problems with one another, we were getting to some nitty-gritty stuff.

Finally, an accountant in the group was frustrated enough to admit why he had a problem with the salesman in the group. His explanation was painfully simple:

**"I don't respect you because you have no qualifications. You're just a salesman".**

There was an awed silence while the salesman went a shade of purple and fought to control his temper.

**"So you don't value people who are in sales,"** came the eventual strangled reply.

**"No"** said the accountant.

In the verbal bloodbath that ensued, the accountant was left in no doubt that he too needed to be in sales.

"Anybody who hasn't yet realised that **everybody** is in sales has a lot of catching up to do."

## How to Sell?

- When you talk about the present, put it in the long-term context so that people can relate the significance of their actions now to what will be or could be.

- Talk about the future in a way that makes it clear how excited by the opportunities you are, always making sure that you point out how it will be of benefit to your team.

- Take whatever steps are necessary to ensure that everyone is aware of not only what is expected of them, but why, so that everybody has a clear understanding of their purpose and personal contribution to overall success.

- Encourage everybody at any level to ask questions about the direction of the business or function, and be as full and open in your answers as you can possibly be.

- Deliver a consistent message to everybody, and be careful to maintain your level of personal enthusiasm.

- Practice your sales pitch by trying to enthuse anybody who will listen about what you are trying to achieve.

- Hold individual meetings with your team members with the specific intention of leaving them feeling enthused, and with a greater personal commitment.

- Look for opportunities to sell whenever you can. Make the message consistent, but don't be a cracked record. Always look for new ways to sell.

- If you've never done one, go on a selling skills programme. It might revolutionise your outlook!

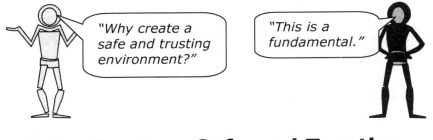

"Why create a safe and trusting environment?"

"This is a fundamental."

# Why Create a Safe and Trusting Environment?

Few people expect a working environment where they are guaranteed a job for life. Most recognise that organisations constantly resize and cut back on even their most senior executives. So why "stick your neck out" when it could be dangerous?

This fear factor has the potential to ensure that there is little challenge of the status quo or risk taking that could result in tremendous reward for the business. It can actually prevent the "thinking" discussed earlier.

If a leader creates an environment in which the team is confident that — economic conditions not prevailing — they will be supported whilst they continue to give their best, they will be able to contribute without fear of reprisal, and so be prepared to give more.

If the team has confidence in the leader and their abilities, they feel safe in the knowledge that the best is being done for the business, and thereby, their futures.

Trusting in the leader has a great deal to do with their technical knowledge and management process skills, for what else is there to judge them by initially? However, as relationships develop, the extent to which a team feel that their leader is worthy of trust on a personal basis will have an enormous impact upon their willingness to give their best.

When people consider that they are being dealt with in a "straight" manner, they feel more confident in the future even if they know that there are bad times ahead. When you know that you can trust somebody, and you don't have to be concerned with their integrity in dealing with you, you respond to them accordingly.

*"Constant change in today's organisations can leave people a little in the dark: great if you like it, scary if you don't.*

*The leader who can create a safe and trusting environment is making sure that the lights are left on, just in case."*

I see many management boards where there is a reluctance to challenge. In some cases it's because the CEO is too intimidating an autocrat to allow dissent. In others it's because the members are too polite to want to risk open conflict. Or in others, they are recoiling from previous instances where conflict has left them at loggerheads and unable to work together for months. One way or another, they do not have a safe and trusting environment.

I was asked to work with one such group in America where they were suffering from every single possible cause! Prior to making an intervention, I interviewed all of the board members and found one common feature: the grief about their situation was palpable, and they all saw it as their CEO's responsibility to create a safe and trusting environment for them.

When I met the man himself, I found that he was acutely aware of the issues, but like the vast majority of top people, had never had the training in facilitation techniques that would enable him to deal with the issues after the fact.

When I got the whole group together, the board members seized the opportunity — explicitly or implicitly — to lay the blame at the CEO's door and, in truth, he did need the feedback. But when I'd given them the time to "get it off their chests", I made sure that they all got some feedback about the need for them to grow up a bit and recognise that dynamic tension in the workplace is actually an asset. It only becomes a threat if it is personalised in the way that they had just delivered it.

The session was very productive, but on an on-going basis, the most important point that they bought in to was this one: To create a safe and trusting environment is everybody's responsibility, and there is no reason why all members of a team shouldn't be taking steps to ensure that such an environment arises.

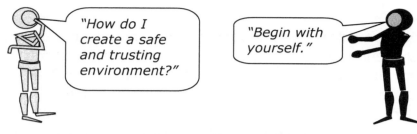

# How to Create a Safe and Trusting Environment

- Encourage and verbally reward challenge. Be frank with your team and allow them to speak their minds freely in return.

- Ask for personal feedback from individuals in private so that they have the opportunity to raise issues with you that they may be reluctant to raise with colleagues present. If you receive no feedback you're either a brilliant leader already, or you don't have a safe and trusting environment.

- If you receive criticism be open and positive in responding to it. Try to avoid rationalising your actions unless you believe that the *circumstances* surrounding your actions are not clear — not your *behaviour* itself.

- If you propose to take action on feedback make it clear what it is and ensure that progress is monitored.

- Take steps to ensure that all members of your team are "heard", and that everyone has the opportunity to voice their opinions when appropriate.

- Take action to be protective and supportive of staff when necessary. Loyalty breeds loyalty.

- Try to behave in a way that is unthreatening to others, always using effective management styles.

- If you state you have an open door policy, make sure that you do!

- Allow sufficient time to hear people's point of view thoroughly, or if there isn't time, set another meeting.

- Avoid cancelling meetings wherever possible. It makes people feel that they are low on your priority list, and unimportant.

- Make sure that your team or sub-managers are doing the things outlined above. The integrity of your approach can be undermined by theirs.

## Why Offer Autonomy?

When you have people around you who are naturally proactive and motivated, experience demonstrates that the more freedom that you give them, the higher the return you are likely to get. Giving autonomy (often described as the buzz word "empowerment") is based on this notion that a free rein engenders ownership, and stimulates thinking skills that reap greater organisational reward.

True autonomy would represent a potentially dangerous management strategy because of the maverick nature implicit in unbridled actions. It almost works on the basis of the higher the risk the higher the reward.

But offering autonomy is often misunderstood, and claimed by managers who are merely delegating.

Under the guise of empowerment, it's also a vogue for businesses — that by their very nature can't give the unbounded authority that goes with autonomy — to claim that they are empowering organisations. They do it because they want to promote ownership of responsibility.

But at management level it is far easier to offer autonomy, by demonstrating such a high level of trust and confidence in your people, they almost feel an obligation to deliver a return. It becomes their duty to fulfil your trust.

However, be aware that for the vast majority in the workplace, the expectation of an unspecified and unlimited return can be onerous and intimidating. It is far simpler to just do what you are told. That is why it is only something that can be offered. You cannot impose autonomy.

Only those who want autonomy will give you a return if you offer it to them and give them the kind of freedom that the word implies.

In a previous role, I identified a need that was unfulfilled.

I took the issue to my boss who seemed somewhat frustrated to be presented with what could be a very troublesome issue.

He asked me what I thought should be done about it, but as I hadn't really given it enough thought I couldn't give a decent answer. He sat and regarded me for a while, and then said *"Is this something you want to deal with?"*

I replied in the affirmative.

*"OK"*, he said, *"Do whatever you think is appropriate, and let me know how you deal with it."*

Scarcely able to believe my ears, but never one to miss an opportunity, I left in a hurry before he could change his mind.

Months of research and planning followed, and all the time, I was free of any checking or reporting that I would have perceived as interference. When all was ready, a presentation was made to senior management that was little more that a cursory sign-off, and the project got underway.

The end result was a stunning success, and the problem was solved.

I felt immense gratitude to that manager for showing such trust and giving me such freedom, and he was able to capitalise on the success of the project by espousing the value of his enlightened management techniques!

I can't in all honesty say that he began with the best of intentions, but I am sure that the end result provided some useful learning for both of us.

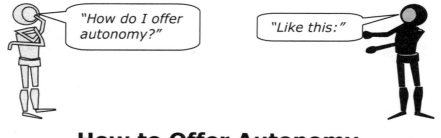

# How to Offer Autonomy

- Recognise that autonomy in its truest sense is not something that you can necessarily give. However, making others feel autonomous by making their contributions as uninhibited as possible is a good start.

- As you sell, make it clear to all that you expect and welcome contribution outside the confines of a job description. Don't leave them with the impression that you're asking for more for the same money

- Make sure that everybody is aware that progress in business depends upon personal initiatives just as much as business ones.

- Clarify the levels of freedom you are able to give to your team in achieving results, and try to impose as few restrictions as possible.

- Avoid restricting yourself by feeling that you have an obligation to comply with precedent. Remember that at some point somebody actually created those precedents, and that new ones can also be brought into existence.

- Demonstrate through your words and actions the confidence that you have in individuals — it will help develop theirs.

- When you receive new and valuable ideas , ensure that they are acted upon and that everybody is aware of what is happening.

- Welcome and celebrate it when the business does profit from initiative. Never be afraid to make a fuss of someone who has given a good return to the business because it will encourage others who want the same praise.

- If individuals whom you have given autonomy to let you down, don't over-react and withdraw freedoms. This is a knee jerk response that will disillusion everybody.

- Try to engender an ethos that makes people feel that they are also owners of the business, and that "we're all in it together".

## Why Train and Develop?

The benefits of training and development per se are fairly obvious: the more people are developed, the more they are able to offer.

However, the threats of not providing for individual's training and development relate to the development of the thinking skills deficit we talked about earlier. If it is not provided for, the risk of ineptitude threatens the whole business.

T&D is in part about equipping individuals with the skills and mindset to "play the game to a higher level". So who better to equip them with those attributes than the current holder of that position?

Learning is something that is valued by the majority of individuals who possess the ambition that has taken them to management positions, because they realise that it profits them to receive it.

The expectation of how we will receive it tends to revolve around formal training courses, home based study, day release etc. But we almost expect formal training as of right from the workplace.

Therefore, if an individual takes the time to do something, or provide some opportunity that extends our learning, our relationship with that individual changes. They assume a higher level in our personal perception because they have given us something that is of value. Respect and loyalty results.

Thus, if a manager is able to informally train and develop, and others can learn as a direct result of their exposure to that person — even vicariously — that manager's position is partially enhanced to one of leadership.
The role of someone who develops our learning is that of someone who leads us. At the same time, T & D is the very essence of ensuring that the thinking skills deficit does not develop.

*The mystique surrounding development is badly misplaced.*

*All you have to do to develop someone is: identify what you need them to be, determine their shortfall, tell them about it, provide them with a way of correcting the issue, and monitor their progress.*

*Then start all over again."*

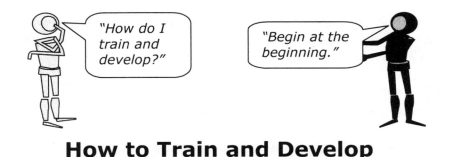

## How to Train and Develop

- Not all training and development issues are as complex as they might appear. Many can be carried out using common sense and good communication skills. Don't start with the mindset that you're out of your league.

- Define clearly what the needs are for a role, plus your expectations from somebody as their manager. Don't rely on a job description to be enough. Expand your expectations to cover attitude, behaviour, values, and all of the broadest possible areas where people can have shortfalls in their development.

- Remember that technical and process development issues tend to be tangible and readily apparent, but it's in the other areas of the development pyramid where more guidance is often needed.

- Take the time and trouble to give one-to-one feedback to your team on how they could improve their performance. Don't restrict what you say to *your* areas of comfort. Consider *their needs* in the light of all of the issues covered in this book and think how they could benefit from some of the learning points.

- Set aside specific time slots to discuss and understand each individual's personal thoughts about their development. What do they want from their careers, and how can you best help them to achieve it?

- At periodic intervals, review the way individuals have developed with them. Provide evidence wherever possible, and look at the steps that they will need to take in order for them to achieve their goals.

- Explain the rationale of business decisions to those who weren't party to them. It will enable them to increase their understanding of how "business" works and help prepare them for responsibilities they might hold in the future.

- Share the benefit of your experience by discussing the way in which tasks or projects could be carried out. Be careful to avoid being seen as a know-all, and keep your suggestions discussion based. Suggest, don't impose.

- Wherever possible, extend the range of a person's experience by involving them in meetings or projects that would not normally be a part of their role.

- Coach your team in management techniques and approaches, demonstrating wherever possible. If you can't do this yourself, bring in a development professional who can.

I've worked in many organisations where directors are described as glorified managers. And managers as doers, or go-fors.

I've had Chief Executives bewailing their woes about the lack of talent to provide for succession planning.

More bizarrely, I've even seen an organisation where the importation of "thinking" talent was such a threat to the existing management that several newcomers were actually forced out within months of their arrival. They lost some seriously good people.

These are simply features of the "Doing/Thinking" problem. The issue is a fairly straightforward one to address if businesses are prepared to invest the time and money in equipping managers with the skills, knowledge and experience that fall in these gaps.

How many times have you seen your organisation go outside to recruit for a position rather than fill it internally?

Outsiders definitely bring fresh perspectives, but they're expensive too. They usually want more money, and there's a lead-time before they can understand the new culture and how to perform effectively. Most senior managers I've talked to reckon that this lead-time is upwards of a year.

All this being the case, wouldn't it be more cost effective to invest in the internal candidate who might have been suitable for the job, who didn't quite get it because they didn't have the right experience, but who was knowledgeable about and loyal to the company? And who's now really demotivated.

Just one more thought about that outsider: people generally move up to progress their careers, not sideways. Therefore it's a progression for the outsider too. That might well mean that in their old job, they were at the same level as the person you passed by.

So was it really necessary to bring in an expensive stranger?

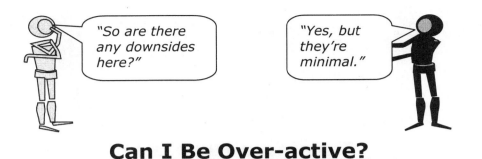

# Can I Be Over-active?

Later on we'll use the phrase "Any strength overplayed becomes a weakness" and something similar applies here. We've already alluded to some of them, but just be aware of these potential danger areas:

## Visibility

In your attempts to ensure that you are recognisable as the leader, don't get caught up in your ego. Visibility is only in part about marketing, so always ensure that there's a good reason for publicising yourself.

## Sell

Take every opportunity to sell, but don't let them feel like you're ramming it down their throats. Be subtle and try to combine your selling efforts with attempts to be visible. Vary your approach to avoid coming across like a cracked record.

## Create a Safe and Trusting Environment

A safe and trusting environment is a fine thing, but never let it develop to the point where individuals lose their drive and become complacent.

## Offer Autonomy

Watch out for the potential for too much autonomy to create "in-fighting". It often unleashes ambition and determination, which is a good thing, but the unscrupulous may start to disregard one another. Ensure that it comes within a strong framework of team working.

## Train and Develop

This can be extremely time consuming and often leads to a demand for more. This is not a problem unless you are the central focus for developing others. Find a balance in your time between not giving enough and giving too much. As an opposite extreme, avoid thinking you can do it once a year.

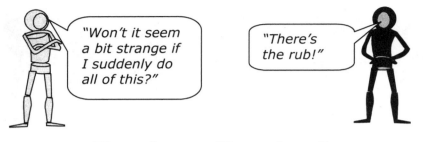

# Turning a New Leaf

You don't necessarily have to do all of these things at once, but do be aware of the interdependent nature of these actions.

For instance, it's almost impossible to **Sell** without **Visibility**. People aren't usually that receptive to **Train and Develop** without a **Safe and Trusting Environment**. And so on.

Depending upon your personal circumstances in the workplace, not all of them may be wholly appropriate anyway. **Offering autonomy**, for instance.

What I'm saying is that these five particular things — that lead to a whole host of actions — will encourage people to follow you. If they perceive the suddenness of you doing them as insincere, remember what we said earlier about **Learning to Lead**.

It may well be unwise to overpower your team with a wave of new techniques theories and ideas, but hopefully you'll already be doing at least some of these things.

> **If you're not, you should be!**

Just ensure that you keep them in your mind and look for opportunities to "slip them in". What you will find is that the more you do them, the more people will like it and want and expect more.

You committed to going the whole way over a hundred pages ago, so don't back out now.

# In Summary . . . .

- To be a real leader I need to take actions that managers don't.

- They will take extra effort, but reap great rewards.

- Broadly summarised, the actions are:

  - **Be Visible**
  - **Sell**
  - **Create a Safe and Trusting Environment**
  - **Offer Autonomy**
  - **Train and Develop**

- There are a whole host of sub-actions that I can take to ensure that I am doing all of these things.

- Each action adds value to the person who is the recipient of it, and is — as such — a motivator.

- All of them are equally valid, but not all situations will require me to do all of them.

- If I am to be a real leader I need to be conscious of the need to do all of these things, but they should be delivered in a way that is spontaneous, not contrived.

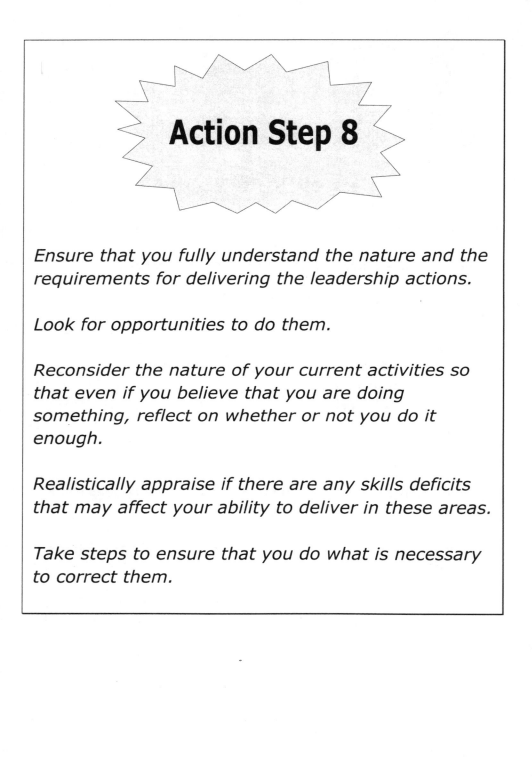

# Action Step 8

*Ensure that you fully understand the nature and the requirements for delivering the leadership actions.*

*Look for opportunities to do them.*

*Reconsider the nature of your current activities so that even if you believe that you are doing something, reflect on whether or not you do it enough.*

*Realistically appraise if there are any skills deficits that may affect your ability to deliver in these areas.*

*Take steps to ensure that you do what is necessary to correct them.*

**9**

# Leadership Persona

- ✗ In many ways, the way a leader **IS**, is just as important as what they **DO**.

- ✗ Certain qualities are universally attractive and pivotal in promoting followership.

- ✗ They can all be developed, and if delivered in the right balance, take you a long way towards being a leader.

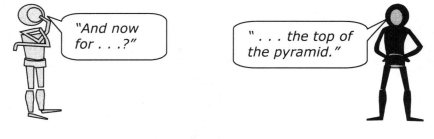

# A Leader's Persona

The last phase in becoming someone that others will want to follow is the persona that you exhibit.

You could call this all sorts of things, but what I'm basically describing is the ability that you have to make an **impact** on and **influence** other people, simply as a result of who you are, and the way you manage yourself.

**In other words, your ability to create an emotional response in someone else that causes them to want to follow you.**

Of all of the things that we've discussed, it's by far and away the most difficult, but it reaps the greatest rewards in terms of the loyalty you can create in others and the willingness it creates for them to do things just for you.

Some people call it the personality factor, some call it charisma. It's probably all the same thing, but I call it :

> # LEADERSHIP PERSONA

The idea of there being a set of attributes that are part of an individual's unique persona, that are key in creating a desire to follow is not a comfortable notion for everybody.

I came across an organisation that thrived on strict adherence to its hierarchy. It ran with near military precision, and prided itself on the technical expertise of its managers, and their abilities in the areas of management process. And these were indeed, without question, excellent.

The organisation operated in several different locations throughout the world, and having been immensely successful, was running into some problems with changing staff expectations.

It was clear from a neutral observer's perspective that they were going through the exact model of difficulty prompted by change, as expressed in "The Need to Lead".

I was engaged to develop leadership skills in their most senior managers. On a particular event where I was attempting to do just this, all went well until we got to the issue of leadership persona, at which point discomfort rippled around the room. About half of the audience started to criticise the idea, and got quite aggressive about it.

I thought that the reason for their argument was pretty obvious, but I wasn't going to face them with it, and I had the confidence of the knowledge that this stuff really works, so I didn't back down. A heated argument developed between those who agreed and those who didn't.

Then one man suddenly shouted: ***"The only reason you lot don't like hearing this stuff is because you're scared. You're afraid that you won't be able to do this, and you can't stand the idea that there's anything more needed than your titles to get the job done."***

His tone became more sympathetic. ***"Don't write yourselves off. At least give it a try."*** Nobody spoke for a long time, then one by one the doubters started to nod their heads in agreement.

I don't know yet if they'll all be successful in developing as leaders, but those few seconds were a revelation. They were a revelation to those managers who suddenly had to face up to the truth about themselves, and that kind of honesty with yourself is a good start.

# Intangible Made Practical

To say that the qualities of a leader's persona are indefinable is akin to the "leaders are born not made" theory.

If leaders are born, how come when a new baby comes into the world the doctor never says "**IT'S A LEADER!**"?

Simply because we can't tell who has these qualities at the time of birth. That means that they must developed as you grow up. If you ever watch children playing in a school playground, you can spot the leaders there.

And since children don't have the power structures of an organisation or any of the other things that we've talked about that tell them who they should be following, how do they know who to follow?

Simple. They're following the person who has already started to develop a leader's persona.

Children start to develop the qualities of leadership persona at a very early age. Some do, some don't. Some will lose them later in life. But if we could study and define the specific qualities of a leader's persona, we could also learn to do these things.

And that's exactly what I've done, and here are the qualities:

## *Qualities of a Leader's Persona*

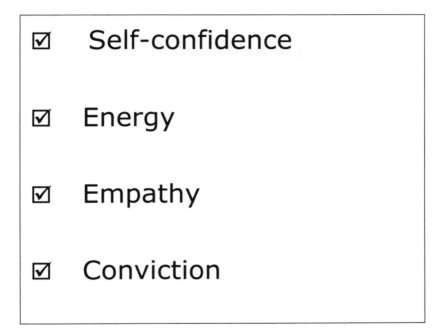

☑　 Self-confidence

☑　 Energy

☑　 Empathy

☑　 Conviction

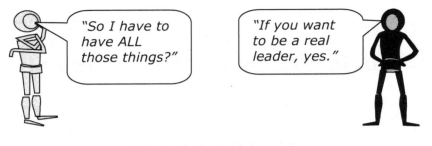

## Total Persona

Don't be too concerned. It's not as bad as it sounds.

For a start, you may possess lots of them already, but the trick here — unlike with the leadership actions — is to be all of them, all of the time. The balance of achieving these qualities and the behaviours that flow from them is vital.

You cannot afford to be excellent in some areas and weak in the others because that would potentially mean that you had both extremes of behaviour, and weaknesses — at the same time.

Persona attributes are almost all about what others perceive you to have as facets of your character, that they judge through your actions.

A lot of them are simply about professionalism and self management, and understanding the potential that is inherent in these things. They may also involve subsuming some of your own needs for the greater need of those you seek to lead.

Thus, in many respects, adopting the persona of a leader comes back to the acting we discussed in "Management Impact".

In fact, as you will see, persona and impact are inextricably linked. This shouldn't be a problem for you because you've already started to work on your development, so let's look at these issues one-by-one.

"A real leader's behaviour becomes a mask for their personal feelings."

One of the finest business leaders that I have encountered had a reputation both inside and outside his business that made him into a superman.

One morning, whilst preoccupied with important matters, he entered the office and strolled across the open plan floor failing as he did so, to speak to absolutely everybody that he encountered.

The rumours and gossip spread like wildfire.

Such and such had upset the leader.
The leader was in a bad mood.
The leader was worried.
Things were going wrong.
The business was in trouble.
The business was on the verge of collapse.

Within hours he was faced with a deputation of worried staff who, in line with the company's openness policy, had come to ask to be put out of their misery.

It sounds like an exaggeration, but it really happened.

The message is a powerful one: when you are a real leader people place an immense amount of store by your behaviour and actions. You are on show all of the time, and your professionalism needs to become a mask for any personal feelings that you may have.

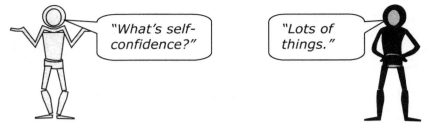

# A Leader's Self-Confidence

Of all of the persona attributes, self confidence is really the most important because it underpins all of the others, and it's absence negates the value of the others. If you don't have it, people simply won't follow you.

Followership requires you to place your trust in someone else. If you trust someone in this context, you must also have confidence in them. If they don't have confidence in themselves, why should you have confidence in them? Therefore why would you follow them?

Confidence is something that we perceive in others as a result of the way they're communicating with us. In the workplace, that comes down to three principal actions:

**Assertiveness**

The willingness and ability that you demonstrate to stand up for your own beliefs, values, ideas and rights, in a way that demonstrates your respect for the rights of others.

**Deportment**

The way you carry yourself physically that sends a message to others concerning your own beliefs about your self worth. The conclusions that others would draw from just observing your body language that would tell them how you feel about yourself.

**Involvement**

The ability and willingness to proactively involve yourself and contribute to discussions at any level. Your willingness to put yourself at risk by exposing your own ideas and make contribution through challenge.

"How do I develop self-confidence?"

"With more ease than you might think."

# Developing Self-Confidence

Your level of self-confidence may be something that was determined way back in your childhood. However, you can think of it as existing in two ways: inner and outer self-confidence. That which you feel inside yourself, and that which other people see.

For the purposes of persona, the one that is most important is outer self-confidence. It doesn't actually matter that much what you feel inside, providing everybody always sees confidence on the outside.

This is because confidence is something that we perceive in others. We don't actually know for certain whether it's there or not, but we form judgements about it based on the evidence of our contact with a person.

To develop outer self-confidence is therefore a matter of displaying the qualities that we've already discussed, because these are the key areas around which people form their judgements.

If you can't do them, start acting.

Inner self-confidence is a bit more tricky to develop since it might mean overcoming years of issues relating to self belief. However, outer acting is a good place to start since — like the natural you may become the developed you — if you act well enough, you'll feel it too.

People who are speaking in public tell you that they were terrified, but they never looked it. Then they do it often enough and they're no longer intimidated.

However, if you wanted to do something more radical to affect your level of inner self-confidence, there are some excellent self-help materials available these days.

I've lost count of the number of managers I've come across who have had problems with their own levels of self-confidence. Sometimes it's obvious; sometimes they hide it very well; often they compensate for the lack of it by appearing overly confident, or downright aggressive — a front that doesn't do them any favours.

When I see self-confidence issues during a development programme, I always wonder if the individual will come to me at the end for help with it, and they often do. But during one such event, I witnessed the actions of a director who acted at all times with tremendous assurance, even delivering a presentation to an audience of outsiders with considerable aplomb. I had no doubt that I wouldn't be discussing his level of self-confidence.

However, much to my surprise he requested a one-to-one to discuss that very thing. Even more unexpectedly, during that session he broke down in tears and expressed his very deep concerns that he would be found out. His position was business critical and he felt himself to be "living a lie".

We talked at length and he revealed some of the background that had created his perceived shortcoming, but it was too deep to tackle in the brief time that we had. I was able to reassure him that his outer self-confidence was impeccable, and he took comfort in this fact. I was also able to recommend a variety of materials that I knew from experience others had benefited from, and the last I heard of him, he was getting on famously and was coping with himself.

What this demonstrates is that it IS possible to get to the top on the basis of outer self-confidence. Obviously it's much more comfortable if you feel it inside to, and owning up to a lack of self-confidence is a good way to start dealing with it. There is a danger that one day it will somehow "pop out" when you least need it to. But irrespective of this, take heart from the fact that there are many very senior people who have the exact same issues.

# Appearing Self-Confident

- Try to cultivate an "air" of self-confidence and ensure that this never strays into arrogance.

- Always present a "professional" image. This includes paying attention to your dress and personal appearance, since these are also sending out messages about you.

- Avoid taking any actions that might be interpreted as unprofessional.

- Observe yourself or get feedback from others about your physical impact and remember that in the eyes of others, the outer is reflecting the inner.

- Initiate and propose new ideas, and ensure that you don't keep those ideas to yourself.

- Put forward your ideas at the highest level possible, and even though you may feel it, don't let it show if you feel intimidated.

- Make sure that you stand up for what is important to you, or what you can see is important to the business, and don't back down under pressure.

- In the process of standing up for yourself, avoid being insensitive or disrespectful. Have the courage to admit when you are wrong — with dignity and good grace.

"*A leader can never have too much self-confidence.*

*But if that confidence ever becomes brash arrogance, you'll no longer be somebody others will follow.*"

# A Leader's Energy

Energy in this context is not just a physical thing. It's mental too. The amount of energy a leader demonstrates has a major impact upon others. They draw strength from it for themselves. It becomes an indicator of what is possible, or even expected. Moderate or low levels are basic expectations, but a high level can lift, inspire and even invigorate.

By the same token, a lack of it can be as damaging as its presence is positive. For a leader who is able to demonstrate high energy levels, if that level falls off, it can easily be misinterpreted. Thus energy needs to be delivered in a way that is physically palpable (merely claiming it is certainly not enough) and consistent.

In the workplace, that comes down to three principal actions:

**Positive Mental Attitude**

Consistent optimism — tempered with realism — about all situations. Your ability to see the opportunities and advantages in all situations , and a resulting manner that is wholly convincing to others.

**Enthusiasm**

An infectious spirit which pervades your mood, and has the ability to rub off onto others. This needs to be tempered with a sensitivity to the mood of others and an acceptance that their level of enthusiasm and drive might be less than yours. It should never become sickening or abrasive.

**Drive**

The ability to keep on going, both physically and mentally, whatever the circumstances or pressures.

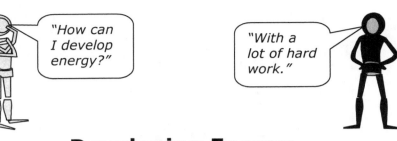

## Developing Energy

A good starting point will always be your physical energy, since it has such a great impact upon your mental energy. Physical energy is almost like a muscle that can be developed to a peak; overworked to the point where it almost appears as a deformity; or not fully utilised and left to go to fat.

To achieve peak performance, all individuals require good diet, regular exercise, and an avoidance of over tiredness. It builds energy levels and helps to combat stress. A healthy body does help to create a healthy mind.

Since everyone is physically different, and this kind of programme has to fit into that person's particular lifestyle, it would be impossible to prescribe a catch-all solution.

Bear in mind that if you do not look after yourself physically, it will be difficult to sustain the kind of high energy output that a leader needs to provide for the needs of others. The kind of energy that can be felt.

Your mental energy obviously suffers when you are tired. It has even been suggested that as you become fatigued, parts of your brain turn off and distort your perceptions.

This can be very dangerous for a leader, so be very careful to avoid overdoing it. The more you develop yourself physically, the stronger you become mentally.

Energy is a quality of persona that almost requires you to be a superman, but even he had to get his muscles from somewhere.

I had the pleasure of meeting a man in Saudi Arabia who was one of the most energetic people I have ever come across.

Although in his fifties, he was positively vibrant in his enthusiasm and drive, and truly infectious with it. He was endlessly entertaining to be with, nurturing in the way he dealt with everybody, and inspirational even in the heat of the desert!

As a devout Muslim, there were many times during the day when his faith decreed that he must pray, and this routine included getting up in the middle of the night. Yet he seemed never to get tired.

I first encountered him in his normal office environment where his team worked with a buzz that wasn't common in the organisation. You could almost sense a lull when he left the room.

During the rather difficult and demanding event that I was there to deliver, he kept up his colleagues' spirits as well as his own, and was able to sustain his output night and day, consistently, for several days.

At the end I felt compelled to ask him if he realised what a hugely positive effect he had on others. He smiled at me and shrugged his shoulders: **"Here it is very important to be energetic. We live in heat that drains our bodies but in our work, our spirit is much more important. My spirit has energy and that feeds other people's spirits, so together we can accomplish much. What use is such a thing without others who are hungry?"**

But what was the source of his energy I needed to know?

Again he smiled at me and gestured upwards. **"Ah my friend, it is from Allah of course."**

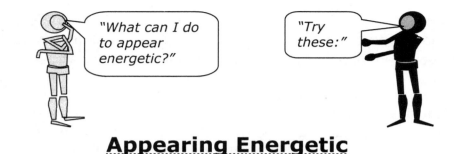

# Appearing Energetic

- Always act in an enthusiastic way, making sure that you are sincere in the attitudes you display.

- Try to encourage others, whilst being sensitive to their needs, and possibly lower levels of energy.

- Show a genuine keenness for your work, and do not let circumstances that are pressured or difficult detract from your consistency of approach.

- Actively look for the opportunity and advantage in all situations. Be quick to point them out to others.

- Maintain optimism and do not allow the pessimism of others to infect you.

- Keep going under physical or mental pressures, and do not demonstrate fatigue, particularly mental tiredness.

- Try to get an awareness of your body's bio-rhythms — it's physical "ups and downs" — and if possible, do your high energy activities on the highs.

- Remember that you can choose your response to any situation, and that a leader's mental energy is based on the evidence of what others experience. The kind of energy that can be felt.

- There's no substitute for actually being energetic!

# *Bio-rhythms and Opportunities*

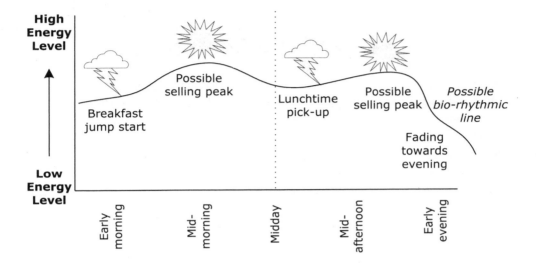

Everyone's bio-rhythms for a day are totally different, so this diagram is only an example of one possibility.

Being aware of yours is the key to recognising when you might be best equipped to perform high-energy activities like selling.

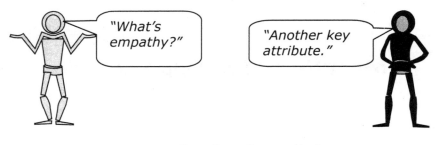

# A Leader's Empathty

First of all, don't confuse empathy with sympathy! Sympathy is going through it <u>with</u> somebody, whereas empathy is understanding what somebody else is going through.

Empathy in the context of leadership involves being able to demonstrate to somebody else that you can understand their perspectives and points of view, and accept their views even if you do not agree with them. It comes back to the points we were discussing earlier about the basic things everybody wants from a communication.

In the workplace, this would involve three principal actions.

---

**Listening**

Listening is the major key to empathy, because it provides the route that enables you to understand the views, beliefs, values and motivations of others. That requires "hearing with attention": listening carefully without distraction, as much for what is not said as for what is. Another fundamental is checking out and questioning what you have heard to ensure that your interpretation matches the speaker's intent. Active listening also requires you to physically demonstrate that you are listening with appropriate body language. Like energy, merely claiming it is not enough. It must be felt.

**Acceptance**

Being able to demonstrate your openness to the possibilities presented by the differing views of others and welcoming dissent.

**Interest**

Having genuine concern for what others have to offer and what you can learn from them; and in what value you can add to them.

---

It's a brave manager who admits to having no real interest in the people in their team. Such an attitude would be suicidal if it became public knowledge, but I have had several managers admit it to me in private.

A fairly typical example is one manager who I was working with in the workplace, who decried empathy as **"*absolute bo\*\*\*\*ks*."** **"*Why should I worry about what my staff think? They're just there to do the bl\*\*\*y job and get on with it*"** she stormed. She then accused managers who were concerned with it of being **"wimps"** for accepting that it was important, and refused to discuss it further.

We were doing on-the-job coaching, so I was shadowing her on and off for several days. Some time after our discussion (and with much ironic good fortune), her boss didn't bother to consider her response to a situation that arose, and basically rode rough shod over her feelings. She was genuinely affronted and upset by the incident, and quick to point out her manager's failing to me when I encountered her very shortly afterwards. We discussed it and I asked what she found unacceptable about her boss's behaviour and what she wanted from him? Slowly it dawned on her what I was getting at, so we revisited the subject of empathy, only this time she was open to the discussion.

It transpired that she — as with many managers with a very high degree of task focus — considered that having to deal with the "human" element was an unfortunate distraction from her true purpose. (This belief is very common in those with a high degree of technical expertise who owe their positions to their knowledge. The point at which they get people responsibilities is the point where the "fun" ends!)

She felt tormented by the issue, since she now understood why the concept was important, but couldn't reconcile it with her other beliefs. After a great deal of fruitless and repetitive discussion, I resorted to a well-tried and tested tactic of suggesting that she might like to read some Taoist philosophy, and recommended a fairly basic, easy to read book on the subject. She reports that it has made a major difference to her outlook, and even made her life easier.

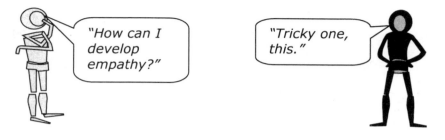

## Developing Empathy

Empathy has it's origins very firmly rooted in a genuine and sincere interest in other people. Whilst you might be able to show it by doing all of the right things physically and saying all of the right things, people will usually spot a sham when they experience it. It comes back in large part to the point about "if you don't show that you care, why should other people?"

There is no easy prescription here, but it might benefit anyone to start thinking about how their own success is measured. Managers are judged by the productivity or success of their teams, and the team is therefore fundamental in determining the manager's level of achievement.

With this as a background consideration, the issues that your team have are ones that should be important to you. Your role as a manager is almost one of an enabler: someone who is able to understand and deal with their issues so that they are able to fulfil the requirements that you have of them.

If you don't have the empathy that enables you to relate to the issues faced in the successful completion of the task, you can't in turn enable them, and if you're not adding value to them in this way, they'll never follow you.

The only way to truly develop empathy is to constantly and consciously be trying to see the other person's perspective. Try and think yourself into their mind.

Or as the American Indian (?!) proverb goes: Try walking a mile in another man's moccasins.

# Appearing Empathetic

- Actively demonstrate that you are a good listener with appropriate body language and responses.

- Do not allow yourself to become distracted when others are communicating with you.

- When it is appropriate to do so, actively show interest in other people's activities by questioning.

- Ensure that you treat everyone equally rather than demonstrating particular interest in some and not others.

- Actively seek to understand other people's motives, and beware of misreading them.

- Demonstrate through your actions and your words that you are open to alternative points of view.

- Avoid giving out signals that others may interpret as coming from a closed mind.

- Show genuine concern and interest in the views and issues that others have.

- Beware of being dismissive of others in any way.

- Actively seek to discover what you can learn from others.

After spending some time working in Japan, I came to leave my hotel for the airport. A cab was arranged for me and at the appointed hour my bags were taken to reception. To my surprise the manager and staff were there to see me off. He asked if my stay had been pleasant and if the staff had served me well. In truth, it was the best hotel I have ever stayed in with exceptional service and personal attention, and I told him so. He bowed to me and then turned and warmly thanked his staff for looking after me. They bowed and almost visibly glowed with pleasure at the praise he had given them.

Then two porters carried my bags to the front door while the manager accompanied me. The doorman opened the door and helped me in to the cab, then ran out into the road and stopped the traffic (on a busy Tokyo street!). As the cab pulled out, I turned to wave, and was met with the sight of the doorman, the porters and the manager all bowing. I felt like royalty and regard the whole experience of staying in Japan as unparalleled in its excellence — mainly because of their behaviour.

I've often reflected upon what that manager was doing. He was empathising with my needs as a customer and making me feel special. He was empathising with the needs of his staff by making them feel valued for their efforts. His praise must have motivated them to provide such excellent service. And his effect on all of us was — in our respective ways — to lead us.

I would go back to that hotel at the slightest excuse — because I've been led in that way — and it is certainly possible to lead customers. And as for the staff, well I can't tell what else went on there, but everything that I saw while I was there suggested that a real leader was in charge.

*"Could you live out this greeting:*

*'I honour the greatness within you.'*

*It's Nepalese, and they do."*

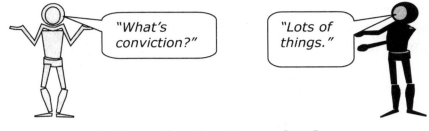

# A Leader's Conviction

Conviction, like energy, is something that other people feed off. Your level of conviction — or lack of it — is like a barometer, providing a measurement of the importance and appropriateness of actions that are taken in the workplace. You often see it described as PASSION.

Remembering that what you say, think or feel legitimises what everybody else is doing, there is a need for demonstrable and consistent conviction if you want similar responses from your team.

However, conviction must be tempered with flexibility and an open mind about other courses of action. To be effective, within the strength of belief implied by conviction, there must exist the ability to recognise if a change in beliefs or actions is appropriate.

In the workplace, this would involve three principal actions:

---

**Tenacity**

A steadfast belief in the correctness of the course of action being followed, and a determination to succeed in the face of setbacks. To be credible, this requires a high degree of resilience, and the display of a balanced emotional equilibrium.

**Commitment**

Your own personal preparedness to do and be seen to do whatever it takes to succeed in bringing about the desired form of success.

**Consistency**

Following a course of action in a way that allows others to see the "common thread" in your approach, and believe in both its, and your, personal integrity.

---

A man who had just been made head of a business unit that formed part of a larger organisation had in many ways been handed a poisoned chalice. The business was failing badly, the workforce were highly demotivated. Despite knowing that the organisation did not really expect a future for the company, or anyone who worked within it, this man was particularly keen to succeed in his first appointment at this level.

In his first week he held a series of meetings with individuals and groups, but even with his management team he found that things were worse than he had imagined. They were dispirited, negative, and in some cases, downright truculent. He quickly realised that turning the business around would be the equivalent of pushing a massive boulder up a very steep hill, and began to wonder if he could count on anybody's support.

(I met him in a social setting after his first week, and he poured out his concerns simply because I was prepared to listen. I was struck by his obvious enthusiasm, but at the time I wasn't really experienced enough to offer any practical advice.)

The next week he gathered his team together and told them how he felt about the business. He acknowledged the problems and the gargantuan nature of the task ahead of them; but he wanted to make it quite clear to everybody that he believed that the business could be turned around. The reaction he got was muted, but it turned to open cynicism when he wrote in huge letters on a white board:

## WE <u>CAN</u> DO THIS

In exasperation he burst out: ***"Look, I really believe this. I'm not just saying it, and if anyone here doesn't, then they'd better leave now."*** Nobody volunteered.

Over the coming weeks he visited the various departments and gave them what was basically the same speech, always ending with **"WE CAN DO THIS".** It became known as his 'battle cry', and he even had some posters put up with the words written on them. In any encounter with his workforce, he never missed an opportunity to make the point, and it became a point of amusement that people would try to get the line in before he did.

Two years later, that business had completely turned around. Today it is one of the most profitable parts of the organisation, and my friend has moved on to bigger things. He's quite modest, but he loves telling a little story about his last day with the company:

At his leaving party, the member of the management team who had been promoted to replace him as Managing Director came up to him and said

*"I just wanted to tell you this before you left: Do you remember the first time you gave us your 'WE CAN DO THIS' speech? Well I had my resignation in my pocket that day, and I was going to give it to you after the meeting. But when I heard you, I realised that you actually believed what you said, and that made me it believe too. I'd never seen anybody with so much conviction about something that had seemed so impossible, and I only stayed because of the things you said that day. That was the point at which I started to believe that we could really do it, and I just wanted you to know the effect that had on me."*

If I were he, I'd want to tell that story too.

"How can I develop conviction?"

"Get convicted!"

# Developing Conviction

Conviction cannot be developed in the same way as the other attributes because you either have it or you do not.

For most people, the issue of conviction comes down to an issue of being true to themselves. However, not having conviction in what you are doing personally, or the way the business is going, can have an extremely destructive impact upon your ability to lead.

Despite all this, displaying it can be relatively easy. Like self-confidence, it very much comes down to what others perceive as a result of the messages you send out.

Conviction is implied most through tonal qualities that others interpret as emotions, like passion. Developing these will reap the greatest rewards.

Of course, the conviction that you have in your head is important, but for the sake of others, acting it out is almost essential.

Ultimately, if you lack conviction, ask yourself "why?"

If the conclusion you come to is a fundamental one, try asking yourself if you're in the right company, or even the right job.

Leaders lacking conviction rarely do themselves or their businesses any favours.

## Appearing to Have Conviction

- Always show determination in the face of setbacks and behave in an emotionally resilient way, never giving way to emotional outbursts or fits of temper.

- Withdraw from a situation only when it becomes futile or inappropriate to progress it any longer. When you do, ensure that others understand your motives for doing so.

- Demonstrate your personal drive and determination to succeed through your words and your actions.

- Never show behaviour that others may interpret as laziness, or do anything that implies a less than totally committed attitude.

- Do not distance yourself from any aspect of a task or situation that you should be involved in, no matter how tedious, laborious or unrewarding you may find it.

- Try to convey to others the common thread and consistency between the actions you take.

- Avoid giving the appearance of being uncertain about objectives or desired outcomes, unless those outcomes have yet to be defined or they require team involvement to assess them.

- Do not show inconsistency in any aspect of your attitude towards either your work or the workplace.

- Act with integrity at all times. Say what you mean and mean what you say.

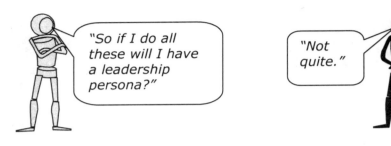

## Personal Persona vs Leader's Persona

The four attributes covered so far might give an individual a certain appeal and charisma in their personal lives.

They are equally important in the workplace, but a vital element is missing that makes all the difference between somebody being capable of inducing followership amongst their social circle, and capable of being a leader in the workplace. And that is:

> # VISION

The vision that a leader possesses needs to be their way of describing the direction or course that they see as being appropriate for their business, function, department, team — or whatever.

Since its purpose is to do this, it is a statement of the direction in which the leader is asking others to follow, and as such they will either want to follow that course, or not follow.

If they don't like the vision, or if there's nothing in it for them, they won't follow. And if there isn't a vision at all, what direction are they going in?

An inappropriate vision, or absence of a vision can cause people to buy-out. Therefore the vision that a leader has needs to be capable of buying the team in, giving them an ultimate goal or something to aim for, and holding their interest whilst in it's pursuit.

I once worked in a department where the alleged leader had no vision.

I should have seen the danger signs when I first joined the team because in my first meeting with my new manager, I asked questions like "what does the department stand for", and "how would the rest of the business consider we perform in line with our stated objectives". They were all met with blank looks.

Time went by, and I became increasingly frustrated by our apparent aimlessness as a department. The whole team was extremely demotivated.

So one team meeting (those things that are so often utterly futile and demotivating — well ours were anyway) I hijacked the agenda and demanded that we resolve the issue of where we were going. What was our vision or, more importantly, what was the manager's vision?

**"What do you mean?"** he replied.

**"You know, a vision statement. One of those things that inspires and motivates us,"** I replied. (I always was difficult to manage.)

I was met with blank looks from him, but by this time the rest of the team were quite up for it, so to give an example I wrote a possible vision for our team up on a whiteboard, straight off the top of my head. To the manager's discomfort, the team liked it, and wanted to adopt it.

I left the company in despair not long after — as did several of my colleagues. The vision had not been sponsored or sold, or even understood.

But then you can't really expect managers to know about these things unless they've had some prior exposure to them. Unless they happen to be in management development and supposed to be experts in these matters.

And unfortunately he was.

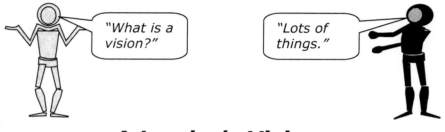

# A Leader's Vision

A vision should really be a device used for the purpose of inspiring the team. It is a future-focussed statement about what is aspired to, and should appeal to people at an emotional level as well as a logical one. It should be meaningful and relevant, and cause people to want to achieve it.

The way businesses usually use them is to make some grand statement about what the organisation seeks to become. The theory is that everybody knows about it, and it buys them in at a personal level. Certainly in large businesses, the reality is that the words are principally intended for the shareholders.

Whatever the size of the organisation, the further down the organisation an individual is, the less meaning a corporate vision has. The "big picture" is often cascaded through glitzy presentations or other impressive communication vehicles that create a good short-term impact.

But as the message is cascaded through the business its impact becomes weaker and weaker. In some cases this is because the commitment to the vision is weaker in those communicating it; in others because the communication simply doesn't take place; but overall it happens because the words become too remote from the reality. For the average employee, becoming "the best whatever it is in the world" has little relevance.

So as well as organisational visions, **ALL** leaders should maintain their own visions that have meaning to their teams, and align with the corporate vision.

There are key vision points within any organisation where somebody needs to have created a vision that is right for that audience. The key points tend to fall between regions, functions, departments, teams and levels of strata within the hierarchy.

The diagram below shows an example, but in practice any organisation could be made up of many more levels and breakdowns.

# *Vision Cascade*

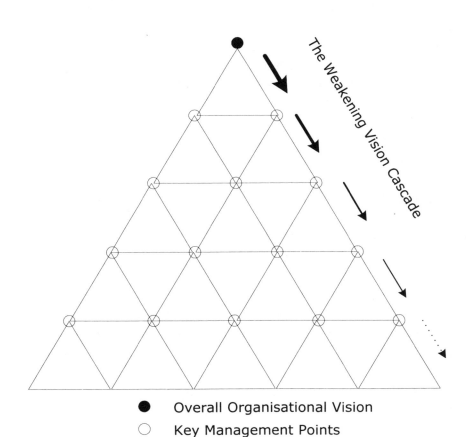

●      Overall Organisational Vision

○      Key Management Points

# Developing a Vision

When seeking to create a vision, work on something that will be meaningful and relevant to both yourself and your people.

Take as its source the range of possibilities, opportunities and impossibilities that present themselves to the business, when considering its future. Make sure that it is exciting, interesting, and gives people something to aim for.

More importantly, it must appeal to the values of those for whom it is intended.

Remember that the vision doesn't have to be created by the leader.

If the highest level of ownership is sought, the team should be involved in its creation.

The leader then needs to be the sponsor of the vision, making sure that their position is used to sell it, and keep using it as the motivational driving force that it should actually be. The vision needs to "live".

It has to be in line with the overall corporate vision, and should pose no threat, nor present any incongruity.

The vision should be fluid and never become a lodestone.
If a vision is unattractive, it will not only fail to persuade others to follow, it will also cause a kind of leadership buy-out.

"What can I do to appear to have a vision?"

"Be visionary!"

# Appearing to Have a Vision

- Don't be afraid to spend enough time considering and weighing alternative courses of action for the business/function. If others consider this "inactivity", make it clear that that is what you are doing.

- Even in times of uncertainty, try to appear to have a clear idea about the direction of the business/function.

- A vision is of no value in promoting followership unless it is shared with those who you seek to inspire with it. People will only recognise a vision if it is communicated, so communicate!

- When you are explaining your vision, make it clear that you have considered the range of possibilities and opportunities that will present themselves in the future.

- Ensure that your delivery of your message, like the vision itself, motivates others.

- Make your vision clear to all, in language that **they** can understand.

- Avoid keeping your ambitions for the business/function to yourself.

- The essence of appearing to have a vision revolves around your ability to sell it to others, and there is very little that needs to be said in this context beyond the things covered in the "How to Sell" section in the chapter "Leadership Actions".

- Recognise that you need to take every opportunity to talk about it, without appearing to be forcing it down people's throats!

"*A vision should be to workers what a lighthouse is to a ship's crew.*

*When it's dark or hazy, there's something to provide a focus and direction, and remind them of where they need to go.*

*When things are clear, it's an irrelevance, but it's still comforting to know it's there.*"

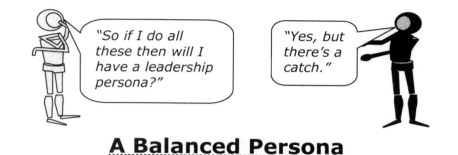

## A Balanced Persona

Like the leadership actions, these issues of persona are totally dependent upon one another. The balance that you need to achieve between them is quite staggering because of the closeness of the relationship between the attributes. For example:

An abundance of **SELF-CONFIDENCE** may damage **EMPATHY**. A lower level of **ENERGY** may be perceived as a lack of **CONVICTION**. Lack of **CONVICTION** may be seen as stemming from lack of **SELF-CONFIDENCE**. And these are just some of the many possible permutations!

The key to their delivery comes down to the skills that you can exhibit in communicating effectively. If you read back over the last few pages, you will soon see that persona is about qualities that others perceive you to have. They can only draw those conclusions from what they see through your behaviour and communication.

As always, it is so easy for an overplayed strength to become a weakness. At the end of the day, persona is the most difficult of the leadership development phases to achieve. Although it is also probably the most rewarding in terms of promoting followership, it is ultimately like beauty, in the eye of the beholder. After all, one person's energetic is another's bumptious.

Bearing this in mind, do not work on some attributes at the expense of others, and be ever vigilant in your assessment of the impact you're having on your colleagues. Try always to act the persona attribute to the extent that the other person needs it, or perceives it as effective. After a while, this becomes easy to spot!

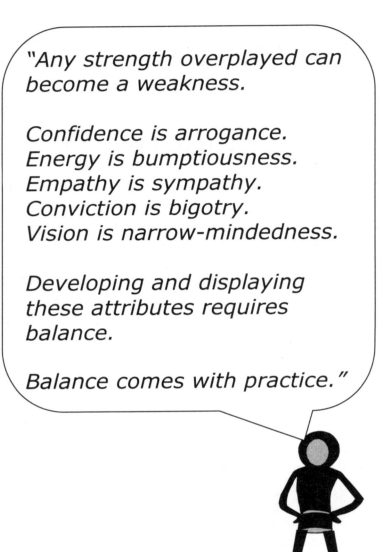

"*Any strength overplayed can become a weakness.*

*Confidence is arrogance.*
*Energy is bumptiousness.*
*Empathy is sympathy.*
*Conviction is bigotry.*
*Vision is narrow-mindedness.*

*Developing and displaying these attributes requires balance.*

*Balance comes with practice.*"

# In Summary . . . .

🖎 Leadership persona is the part of me that I need to use to create an emotional impact upon others.

🖎 The **IMPACT** of **PERSONA** is wholly dependent upon the way that I communicate.

🖎 There is a combination of certain qualities and attributes serve to create the kind of persona that will make others want to follow me.

🖎 They are:

- **Self-confidence**
- **Energy**
- **Empathy**
- **Conviction**
- **Vision**

🖎 Unlike **LEADERSHIP ACTIONS**, I need to display all of these attributes all of the time.

🖎 **SELF-CONFIDENCE** is fundamental, and **VISION** is what makes the difference between people seeing me as a leader in my personal life, and me being able to inspire followership in the workplace.

🖎 The attributes are not illusory qualities, and they can be developed by anyone.

🖎 I need to ensure that my delivery of them is done with balance so as to avoid the danger of the strengths that I have becoming weaknesses.

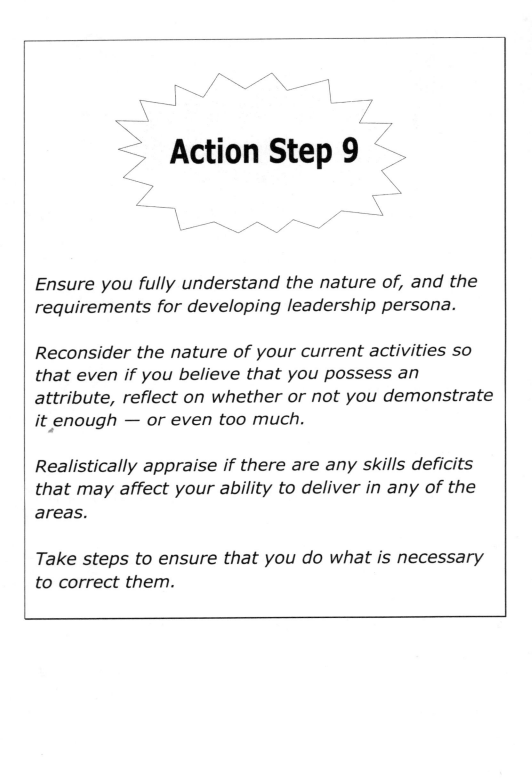

# Action Step 9

*Ensure you fully understand the nature of, and the requirements for developing leadership persona.*

*Reconsider the nature of your current activities so that even if you believe that you possess an attribute, reflect on whether or not you demonstrate it enough — or even too much.*

*Realistically appraise if there are any skills deficits that may affect your ability to deliver in any of the areas.*

*Take steps to ensure that you do what is necessary to correct them.*

## 10

# Putting It All Together

Ø Reading the book has advanced your knowledge about leadership, but it has not necessarily changed you or made you more effective. What you do with the information you now have is what really matters.

Ø All of the phases of development are equally crucial, and all must be attended to.

Ø You may already be a long way there, but the time to start going the final distance is now.

"Do I now know everything I need to know in order to be a leader?"

"Yes. But you need to understand this:"

# Total Interdependence

The interdependence between the levels of leadership development is total. It runs from top to bottom, and bottom to top, and can be seen in any number of "strands". For instance:

☞ A leader who lacks sufficient **TECHNICAL KNOWLEDGE** is unlikely to be able to either feel or exhibit **SELF-CONFIDENCE**. Conversely, who would follow a person whom they perceive lacks either?

☞ The delivery of **LEADERSHIP PERSONA** is wholly dependent upon being able to create effective **MANAGEMENT IMPACT**, because without the latter, the former will be ignored.

☞ Without effective **MANAGEMENT PROCESS** abilities, a credibility gap would develop that would render both **LEADERSHIP ACTIONS** and **PERSONA** largely irrelevant.

☞ What has a leader without a **VISION** got to **SELL**?

To develop as a leader requires ALL of the areas to be worked on. Although they may be tackled in an incremental order, eventual real leadership depends upon doing all of them. There are no shortcuts, or things that are less important than others. Everything that we've covered is of equal importance.

Understanding everything that is written here is of no real consequence. Only your ability to put into practice the things written about in this book matter. As we said right at the start: just reading the book will do nothing except — hopefully — galvanise you.

The BBC showed a documentary some while ago about RAF officers who, as part of their training had to undergo a course in survival behind enemy lines.

In theory, you had to pass the course before you "got your wings", or progressed to the next level of command, or whatever.

The film showed the candidates learning techniques to catch and prepare food, and this included a group learning how to make snares.

A senior officer inspecting their work commented that the snare made by one of the trainees would be pulled apart with very little force from an animal, and that his food would be lost.

The camera then cut away to the trainee responsible for the duff snare to get his comments. He took it quite light heartedly and said something to the effect of **"It doesn't matter if it doesn't work here, provided I understand the principle of the thing".**

I wonder if the principle would matter if he were starving because his snare didn't work?

Would you have considered this individual a "pass"?

To my horror, the RAF did.

Leadership isn't really any different. Merely understanding the principles will never make you a manager others would want to follow.

## It Is All Possible!

So have we been describing unattainable perfection? Is this more than you can cope with? When you see it all arrayed likes this, developing as a leader can appear to be a very daunting task.

But look at it this way:

Many of the skills and attributes that we've discussed you probably already possess. Some may be better developed than others, and you might not have thought about some of the combinations before.

So, make an audit of all of the strengths that you already possess, and cross reference it with your action plans. Get a clear list of what you already have going for you, and what you need to work on.

Combine it all into one working document that will give you a series of action steps to take you all the way to **REAL LEADERSHIP**.

Then if you haven't already started,

# BEGIN TODAY

And as you practice the things covered here, bear in mind this odd truism that we've already alluded to:

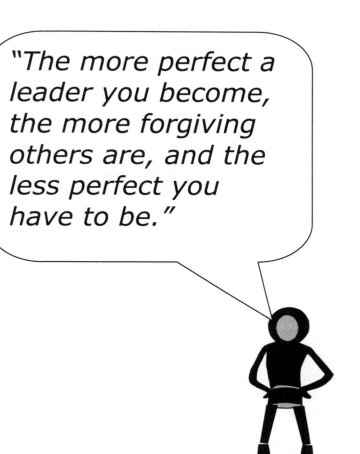

# In Summary.....

- ☒ Businesses all over the world need leaders at an ever-increasing rate.

- ☒ A leader is someone others will follow and give their best for because they want to, not because they have to.

- ☒ Anyone can learn to be a leader if they have the determination and resolve.

- ☒ Leadership development is an incremental process, starting with the technical knowledge and management process skills that every manager has to have, irrespective of their position in the hierarchy.

- ☒ Your personal impact as a manager can either support or undermine your efforts to be effective.

- ☒ Impact that is consistently appropriate to the situation, coupled with the first two levels of development will ensure effective management, but will not make you a leader.

- ☒ You need to take specific actions that add value to others, and behave in a way that suggests a leadership persona.

- ☒ All this needs to be done with balance.

- ☒ **IT NEEDS TO BE DONE TODAY.**

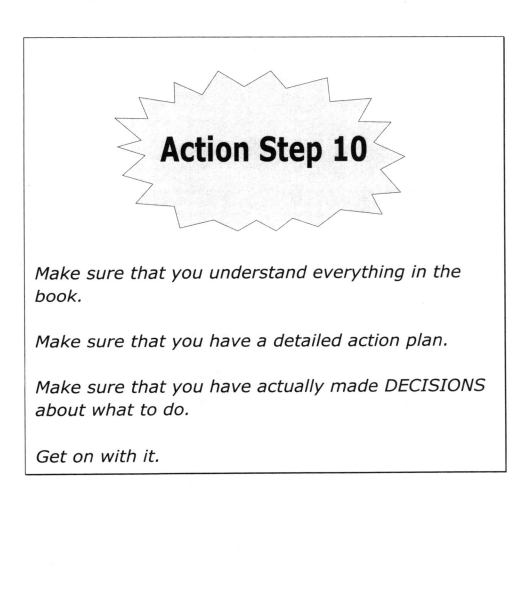

**Action Step 10**

*Make sure that you understand everything in the book.*

*Make sure that you have a detailed action plan.*

*Make sure that you have actually made DECISIONS about what to do.*

*Get on with it.*

# Action Step Summary

## The Need to Lead

- Decide that you will be a leader, and that you will commit to doing whatever it takes to achieve that.

- Don't try to do it. Try means that you haven't decided.

## Learning to Lead

- Understand the phases of learning and DECIDE that you will keep an open mind about what you have to learn.

- Take steps to discover your blind spots.

- Commit to taking notes and developing action points.

- Start preparing others for the changes you intend to make.

## What Leaders Need to Develop

- Reflect upon the development model and the issue of thinking and doing.

- Analyse your own role and assess how much of each you do.

- Consider how much of each you SHOULD be doing and determine what changes you need to make in order to bring this about.

- Dwell upon other managers around you. Can you see evidence of thinking applied? If you can't, it's ultimately your problem too. DECIDE what you are going to do about it.

## Leadership Fundamentals

- Make a review of your technical knowledge base. Assess how up to date it is, and examine it's relevance against what you seek to achieve for yourself in the future.

- Look at the suggestions of the things that leaders need to have knowledge of, and determine where there are shortfalls in your knowledge.

- Make a comprehensive list of the information you need to acquire to ensure that your technical knowledge is everything it should and could be.

- Identify as many sources as you can that will provide you with the input you require, not forgetting the following:

| | |
|---|---|
| Trade Journals | Open University Courses |
| Colleagues | Evening Classes |
| Seminars | Formal Training Courses |
| Libraries | The Quality Press |

- Commit to a realistic timetable, one that will work for your lifestyle, that will allow you to grow your technical knowledge in line with:

☞ Current Job Requirements
☞ Changes and Developments
☞ Career Aspirations

## Management Impact

- Realistically appraise the impact you make, and look for evidence to support your analysis.

- Track the sources of the beliefs and values you hold about the way to lead by reflecting upon the experiences that have shaped your past and determined your present.

- Determine to become aware of the choices that you make, and gauge whether or not you are actively deciding, or just responding.

- Study the communications mix and ensure that you have done enough to equip yourself with the skills and knowledge to make you the expert you need to be in this area.

- Start considering every situation from the perspective of "what should be determining the emphasis of my style?" rather than simply reacting.

## Effective Management Impact

- Make sure that you fully understand the essence of each of the effective styles, and when to use them.

- When circumstances are appropriate, practice using all of the styles until you become proficient in all of them.

- Do not accept the evidence of your own beliefs. Check out your success with those who are the recipients of your management i.e., those upon whom you make an impact.

- Remember that you will need to be proficient in the exhibition of all of the management styles. Even if you don't see the need for all of them right now, eventually they will all feature in your role as a real leader.

## Ineffective Management Impact

- Avoid making the mistakes that turn an effective style into an ineffective one.

- Make sure that you fully understand the essence of each of the ineffective styles, and why the impact occurs.

- Ensure that you do not fall into any of the traps by following the guidance on what not to do.

- Check for possible lapses by requesting immediate feedback from those who are the recipients of your management i.e., those upon whom you make an impact.

## Leadership Actions

- Ensure that you fully understand the nature and the requirements for delivering the leadership actions.

- Look for opportunities to do them.

- Reconsider the nature of your current activities so that even if you believe that you are doing something, reflect on whether or not you do it enough.

- Realistically appraise if there are any skills deficits that may affect your ability to deliver in these areas.

- Take steps to ensure that you do what is necessary to correct them.

### Leadership Persona

- Ensure you fully understand the nature of, and the requirements for developing leadership persona.

- Reconsider the nature of your current activities so that even if you believe that you possess an attribute, reflect on whether or not you demonstrate it enough — or even too much.

- Realistically appraise if there are any skills deficits that may affect your ability to deliver in any of the areas.

- Take steps to ensure that you do what is necessary to correct them.

### Putting It All Together

- Make sure that you understand everything in the book.

- Make sure that you have a detailed action plan.

- Make sure that you have actually made DECISIONS about what to do.

- **Get on with it.**

# Good Luck!

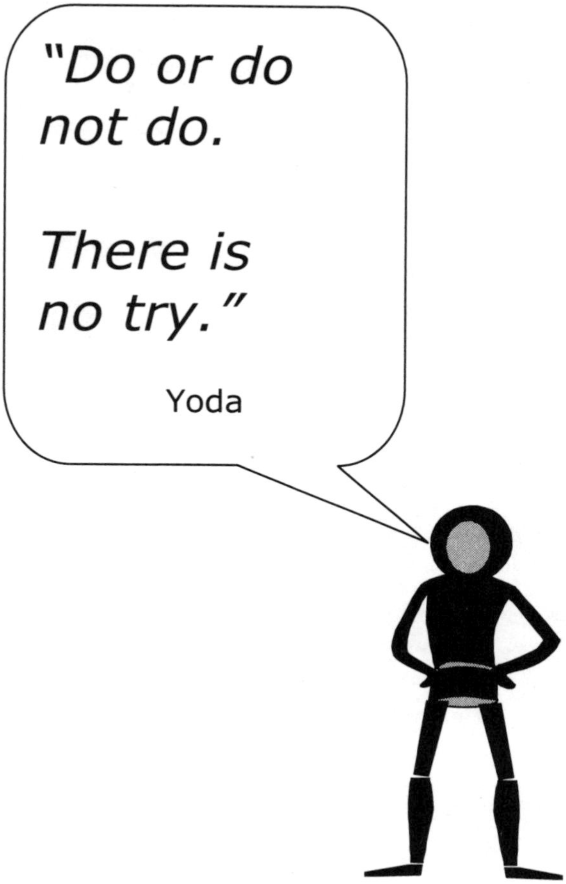
"Do or do not do.
There is no try."
Yoda

## Appendix 1

# How Much of a Leader Are You?

- One of the most important factors in achieving successful development as a leader is to have an understanding of where you are now, and what you need to achieve in order to maximise your potential.

- You can obtain a free profile that will pinpoint precisely the things you need to work on, and allow you to monitor your effectiveness on an on-going basis.

- Regular profiling provides you with proof of your development and brings a host of benefits to you personally, and your organisation.

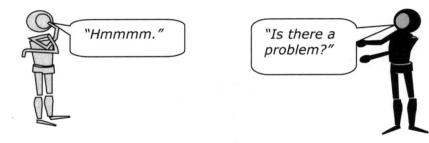

# Knowing Where You Stand

If you've got this far, you will certainly have an appetite for developing yourself, and the question that's bound to be buzzing around in your head is:

**HOW MUCH OF A REAL LEADER AM I?**

Most people want to know simply as a matter of personal curiosity, but there are real benefits in having the answer. Not least amongst these is having information that would enable you to focus your development activities on the areas where you most need them:

You are about to embark upon a process of personal and self-sponsored development. You've probably been in this position before when dealing with other development issues, only this time it's a lot more complex, there's a lot more to do, and there's a lot more at stake.

- You already possess the knowledge acquired from this book about what to do.

- You have personal determination and drive to do something about it.

- If you were also equipped with the information about the specific things that you need to work on in order to improve your effectiveness, how quickly do you think you could turn yourself into a real leader? Probably significantly — i.e. many years — less than it would otherwise be if you were just "shooting in the dark" and trying to better yourself randomly.

So do you want this information?

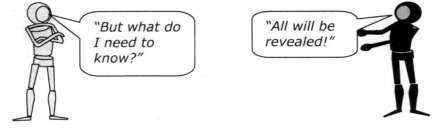

## Vital Information

You need information about all areas of the development pyramid, but some are easier to get than others.

You probably know where your technical knowledge deficits are because they don't take much working out. But have you stopped to review them lately? Remember the advice in "Fundamentals of Leadership" and constantly review your needs, both current and future.

Most workplace appraisal systems are designed to provide feedback on management process skills. They're easy to observe and to develop, so you probably have significant information about these areas.

But the areas where you will have least knowledge are the areas of management impact, leadership actions and leadership persona. You need to know your current level of effectiveness in all of these areas before you can begin to develop them properly.

Specifically this information is:

- **How much of your management impact is effective, and what ineffective behaviours do you use that you need to eradicate?**

- **Against the potential, how much do you do of each of the leadership actions; and are you doing some to the exclusion of others?**

- **In your development of leadership persona, do you take only positive steps, or do you do things that detract from your ability to promote followership. Is your persona developing in the balanced way we've discussed, or are you weak in some areas?**

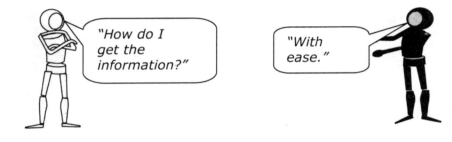

## Getting a Personal Profile

As a developer of others I have an infatuation with maximising the success of development initiatives. When developing leaders, my role is to help them to understand their needs, equip them with the requisite skills, and enable them to be able to prove the results of their efforts. Providing people with a starting point is easy while you're there and can see them in action. It's very difficult when you're not, and monitoring the development of large numbers of people in diverse locations becomes impossible.

So I set about working on a method of profiling an individual that would graphically illustrate for anyone their current state of effectiveness in all of the areas that we've covered, and allow them to monitor their progress on an on-going basis.

Naturally, since effectiveness as a leader is based not on what the individual thinks of themselves, but on their ability to impact upon and influence others, the whole profiling system had to be based around getting feedback from others.

The end result is a unique Internet based system that is totally private and very simple to use. It produces incisive and wholly relevant data, and gives very clear indications of the areas people need to work on. It is available for you to get a personal leadership profile free of charge.

If you contact the email address below, you will receive details of the whole thing, but in the meantime, here's a basic explanation of what you need to do:

- Send an email to the address below to say that you'd like a profile.

- Simply state your name, and the email address that you'd like your profile sent to.

- You'll then receive a an address for data input and a code that will enable three people who you select to give input directly into the computer about you. (The number giving feedback can be extended to as many as you require with full access to the system, but for this first access, we give you a sample of three people's thoughts.)

- All you then have to do is ask your selected people to log in to our site within a specified time limit, and they will be guided through the process.

- Their input will be in response to questions asked on-screen. They can give their feedback at their leisure at any time of day or night.

- The computer that masterminds the operation processes the results. Your profile, containing all of the information we've discussed, is sent straight to you at your email address. It is accompanied by guidelines for interpreting the data, but rest assured that having read the book, the profile will be pretty self-explanatory!

- The data is totally private to you, and is not shared with anyone unless you choose to share it.

- If you want to have the whole thing in hard copy form, either print off the screens that arrive, or specify up front that you'd like hard copy, and give us a standard mailing address for you.

**contact@proactive-consulting.com**

# What Your Profile Shows

**Your Level of Effectiveness of Management Impact**

This model shows the extent to which you use the range of management styles. It is displayed as a pie chart so that you can see in an instant your use of them relative to one another: if 50% of the impact you create is directive, 30% participative and 20% indulgent — or whatever the mix might be.

You'll see if you create all of the impacts discussed, or just some of them. It will enable you to see what percentage of your impact is effective, and what is ineffective. And most importantly, it will give you vital clues as to what behaviours you need to try to do more of, and what less of.

**The Extent to Which You are Taking the Actions of a Leader**

This model, unlike the others, is based on quantity. It shows the frequency with which you are taking the actions that promote followership and displays them as a bar chart.

Because of the way the data is compiled, you can confidently assume that what you are doing in these action areas is effective, but are you doing it enough? From the chart you can instantly determine which of the actions you need to be doing more of, or which skills you need to be developing.

**The Development of Your Leader's Persona**

This model, which perhaps more than any other shows whether or not people are likely to follow you, is displayed in two different fashions.

The first uses a graph that resembles a spiders web (I don't know the technical name for it!) to display the following information:

* Against each of the criteria, it shows the extent of positive and effective actions  that you take that enhance the perception of you having an effective leadership persona.

* Against each of the criteria, it shows the extent of the negative and ineffective actions that you take that detract from perceptions of you as having an effective leadership persona.

* The net effect of these two opposing forces, which is the measurement of the extent of development of your leadership persona.

All of this will demonstrate strengths to play to, and weaknesses to eradicate.

The second, using the same type of graph, is simply the net effect shown against the potential (i.e. the maximum amount of positive leadership persona that others could perceive you to have). It not only displays — very graphically — the extent of persona development, but even more significantly, you will be able to see whether or not you are managing to achieve that all important level of balance between the attributes. If you're not, you'll instantly discover the areas you need to take action on.

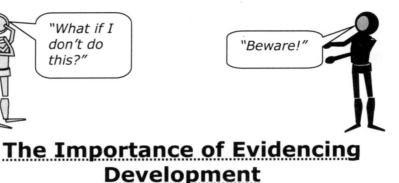

# The Importance of Evidencing Development

Let's be honest about it: most development initiatives go to waste. People undertaking them start out full of enthusiasm and with the best of intentions, and then run out of steam. They may not be getting enough support, or they may be lazy, or they may not care. But the most common reason for this wasteful phenomenon is that people can't see if they're making any progress.

---

**Personal Frustration**

There's nothing so frustrating for an individual than to work hard on personal development, and at the end of the day, never be quite sure, one way or the other, whether or not they're achieving progress.

Inability to see that you are making a difference as a result of new skills and actions causes many to just give up and revert to type. After all, we've already established that developing yourself can mean a lot of hard work.

---

**Organisational Waste**

For an organisation too, this can be a very tricky issue. Many companies spend hundreds of thousands of well intended pounds every year trying to develop their people, but are never able to prove that the expense is justified.

Inability to provide tangible evidence of business benefit often results in development initiatives being cancelled, or just left to die out, denied the all too necessary, but potential time and money consuming follow-on they deserve. All the efforts that have been made are wasted.

"*Success is a spur to greater things.*

*Never miss an opportunity to prove success, and always share the proof with everyone you can.*"

# Data for Personal Development

When you have it, the data will provide you with a remarkable and somewhat unique range of information from which to base your personal development.

- You will have incisive data about your effectiveness that is both relevant, and easily understood. It will reflect precisely the issues we have discussed throughout the book.

- The profile produced will highlight your strengths and weaknesses in all of the areas mentioned. You will see, graphically illustrated, the specific areas in which you need to develop your abilities.

- Because the behaviours identified all have specific development activities related to them, the tools give an indication of activities on which you should be spending your time in order to maximise effective personal change.

- The book is a point of reference so you will also have a tool to assist you in doing just that.

- You can target the specific individual or group from whom you most need feedback. As many or as few people as you wish can be involved on an ongoing basis.

- You can get this information from whoever you choose, as often as you choose.

- By re-running the profile over time, you will actually be able to see whether or not your efforts are paying off. You shouldn't expect instant results, and you should also recognise that development can be a long and slow process. But you will see if you are managing to become a leader!

# Data for Business Development

From an organisational standpoint, the data can offer even more exciting possibilities:

- The profiles provide a rapid and wholly practical method of establishing development needs and highlighting weaknesses, organisation wide.

- A profile is an instrument that can be interpreted without "expert" input, since only an understanding of the simple but powerful concepts we have discussed is required.

- The language in this book provides a vehicle with which to discuss management in a terminology that neutralises the emotion inherent in personal one-to-one feedback.

- The method of gathering the data removes the difficulty many people experience when trying to explain their feelings when giving feedback.

- Profiling supports management development initiatives by proving whether or not the individual has developed as a result. It enables the eradication of costly and potentially fruitless expenditure on training events in these areas.

- The information provided can form part of a regular appraisal process and targets for effectiveness can be set that are actually measured objectively instead of the usual "single manager input" subjectivity.

- An in-house database of profiles can be developed to run normative comparisons. Or reference can be made to the PCI database of all managers profiled to compare.

- The aspect of discovering who are the most effective leaders can be combined with knowledge about experience levels and technical knowledge, and used for succession planning.

- Measurement encourages managers to determine their own personal standards and acceptable levels of performance, irrespective of organisational imperatives. Experience shows that they become driven to improve their performance from testing to testing, and constantly strive for excellence.

A client company of mine was quick to recognise the potential gain for them in profiling their senior management population.

Their managers already had access to the system whenever they felt necessary, but the business decided to replace its traditional performance appraisal system with an annual profiling that would form part of personnel records.

They announced this policy change at a meeting of the entire target population and were met with an instant wave of disapproval and a general chorus of ***"That's not fair"*.**

The Personnel Director who had been making the announcement calmly nodded at the reaction he got and said: ***"OK. If you feel that it's unfair we won't do it. I've got no problem with that, but can somebody explain to me why it's not fair?"***

There was a deafening silence while everybody fought to put into words the reasons behind their discomfort.

The Personnel Director watched with some amusement as one by one, the pennies began to drop, and the managers began to realise that their objections were based on the truth being told about them, and that there would be "nowhere to hide". And once they realised that fact, they couldn't voice it.

***"In actual fact, what we're going to do here is do away with subjectivity and decisions being based purely on who thinks you're a 'good sort'. We're going to create a true meritocracy. Does anybody here have a problem with that?"***

This time a very loud chorus of approval met him.

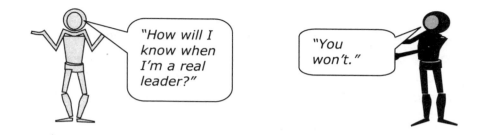

## A Never Ending Journey

If there is a snag in all of this, it's that the journey to becoming a real leader doesn't really have an ending. Anybody who gets to the stage where they believe that they have done enough, that they are the ultimate leader, that they have nothing left to learn, is running into trouble.

The beauty of the system that you've just gained access to is that it doesn't have to be a one off thing. You can get yourself profiled as often as you like. By doing it at least as regularly as once a year, you will start to see changes result because of the development you undertake. Without this kind of feedback, most development initiatives die an early death.

It is possible to score a maximum in all areas of your profile, and I would encourage everybody to strive for that, but that doesn't mean that you've succeeded. Above all else, leadership requires a flexibility in the use of the skills we've discussed. You probably wont always be in the same job with the same people, and even if you were, the needs of the business and your team would change over time. Your leadership must be adaptable.

Hopefully you will get to a point where a profile becomes a health check for you, a way of ensuring that you are continuing to do the right things. But never, ever allow yourself to become complacent. Constantly focus on where you can improve and never accept that you've arrived.

I know two managers from different businesses who were both profiled before coming on a development programme with me (I'll call them Peter and Paul). They were shown their results, worked with considerable determination to understand how to maximise their effectiveness as leaders during the event; and then made great efforts to apply all of the learning on their return to the workplace.

Every six months they were re-profiled and on each occasion, spurred on by their success. Eighteen months later, Peter had achieved a score of 100% effectiveness in management impact, and was strong on leadership actions and persona. Paul was 84% effective on management impact and had a near perfect persona. Although very different people in their own right, both were obviously very strong leaders within their businesses, and both have been promoted.

Then Peter decided that he no longer needed to profile himself. Paul continued to strive for even greater things, re-profiling annually.

Last year, after a gap of two years Peter became concerned that he was losing his touch, so he re-profiled himself. To his surprise and horror, his effective impact had fallen to 72%, and there were significant fall-offs in actions and persona. Paul has consistently improved his effectiveness score, if only by one or two percent on each re-profiling, and has maintained his very high persona level.

When he knew that I was writing this book, Peter asked if I would quote him, so here's his advice:

***"You can never afford to be complacent about your success at leading. You always need to be aware of what you're doing and how well you're doing it. It's a never ending journey, and if you think you can pause for a rest, you'll lose your way."***

# In Summary . . . .

- If I want to maximise my development, it's fundamental that I understand the point which I'm starting from.

- This will enable me to focus on the issues that are most relevant to me.

- By combining this knowledge with my understanding from the book, I can accelerate my development as a real leader.

- A free profile is available to me that will provide specific information about my management impact, leadership actions and leadership persona.

- The profile can be used to bring both personal and business benefits, depending upon how it is used.

- I can actually prove my development by getting re-profiled over time, and ensure that my efforts now do not go to waste.

- The road to becoming a real leader is endless, and even when I succeed, I should avoid the temptation to be complacent.

# Contact the Author

I would be very interested in your reaction to the ideas in this book, or any new thoughts or experiences you might have on the subject of leadership. Here is how to contact me:

Mark Starmer
Proactive Consulting International
Tel: +44 01908 586716
Fax: +44 01908 586716
e-mail: contact@proactive-consulting.com

I look forward to hearing from you.